Mel Bay's

JAZZ
GUITAR
Method

By Ronny Lee

1 2 3 4 5 6 7 8 9 0

COPYRIGHT © 1962, 1963, RENEWED 1990, 1991.
COPYRIGHT © 1993 BY MEL BAY PUBLICATIONS, INC. INTERNATIONAL COPYRIGHT SECURED. ALL RIGHTS RESERVED. PRINTED IN U.S.A.

About the Author

Ronny Lee

Ronny Lee has spent his entire life playing and teaching the guitar. At the age of 16 he was acclaimed an outstanding teenage guitarist and was featured on a weekly radio program in New York City. He later appeared as classical and jazz soloist with various orchestras and also as accompanist to numerous stars.

His realization of the need for an adequate jazz course for the guitar prompted the creation of this book. It is heartily recommend to any teacher of the guitar desiring a thorough, well-graded jazz method.

Foreword

Mel Bay

This is the easiest and most practical approach to jazz guitar I have ever seen. I am sincerely proud to present this method to guitarists desirous of playing jazz guitar as *musicians* instead of fakers.

The Theory Course in Part One can be taught to guitarists possessing an elementary knowledge of the instrument. The Jazz Solo Course should be taken one lesson at a time with the assignments carefully worked out.

2

PART ONE
Solo & Melody Playing/ Improvisation

HOW TO PLAY JAZZ GUITAR

STEPPING STONE NO. 1

NINE STEPPING STONES TO GO

OUR FIRST STEP IN LEARNING TO PLAY JAZZ is to develop an understanding of music theory. To know theory is to possess the tools with which to play jazz.

Whether your jazz preference be progressive or old-time music, rock 'n roll or Dixieland, you will find as you advance through the pages of this book that a knowledge of theory will enable you to apply your abilities toward any jazz form you may desire.

Jazz is based upon chord structure. Chord structure is based upon scales. We will, therefore, start with the study of scales as our first stepping stone toward bettering ourselves musically and learning to play jazz guitar.

Let us think of a long street with little houses on it. The first house we see is Number 1, Main Street. The resident of this house is a family known by the name of "C." A little distance up the street is house Number 2. The resident of this house is a family known by the name of "D." If we continue further up this street, we will see houses numbered 3, 4, 5, 6, 7, and 8. The families in these houses are respectively named E, F, G, A, B, and C. The gentleman named "C" in house Number 8 is a cousin of Mr. C in house Number 1. They are relatives bearing the same name.

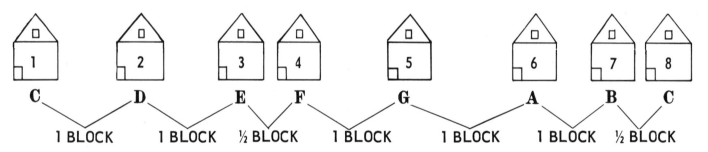

Observe that houses 3 and 4 (E and F) and houses 7 and 8 (B and C) are closer to each other than the other adjacent houses. Actually, these houses are one half block apart. All the other houses are one block apart.

On the guitar as well as on other musical instruments, the notes E and F and the notes B and C are physically closer to each other than are any of the other natural notes. Let us therefore say that the notes E and F are one half step apart; and the notes B and C are one half step apart. All other natural notes are one step apart.

C-D is one step apart

D-E is one step apart

E-F is one half step apart

F-G is one step apart

G-A is one step apart

A-B is one step apart

B-C is one half step apart

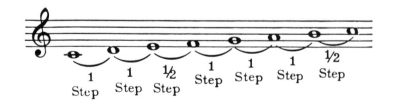

If we were to play the notes C, D, E, F, G, A, B, and C

in ascending order, we would be playing a C major scale.

The C major scale is a group of notes starting on C and proceeding through the musical alphabet until the note C reappears.

Because the notes E and F are one half step apart and since these notes are the third and fourth notes of the scale, we may say that the third and fourth notes of the C major scale are one half step apart. The same holds true for B and C, which are the seventh and eighth notes of the C major scale.

1-2 is one step apart

2-3 is one step apart

3-4 is one half step apart

4-5 is one step apart

5-6 is one step apart

6-7 is one step apart

7-8 is one half step apart

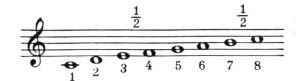

Many music theorists use the phrase "half tone" or "semi tone" for "half step," and "tone" or "whole tone" for "one step." Because the phrases "half step" and "one step" are more commonly used by the professional musician, we will use this terminology. However, all the above phrases are equally correct.

We are now familiar with the notes in the C major scale, and we know where the whole and half steps appear in the C major scale.

ASSIGNMENT

1. Which note is one half step higher than B? _____
2. Which note is one half step higher than E? _____
3. Which note is one half step lower than C? _____
4. Which note is one half step lower than F? _____
5. Which note is one step higher than F? _____
6. Which note is one step higher than C? _____
7. Which note is one step lower than B? _____
8. Which note is one step lower than E? _____
9. Which note is two steps higher than C? _____
10. Which note is two steps higher than F? _____
11. Which note is two steps higher than G? _____
12. Which note is two steps lower than E? _____
13. Which note is two steps lower than A? _____
14. Which note is two steps lower than B? _____
15. Which note is one and one half steps higher than D? _____
16. Which note is one and one half steps higher than A? _____
17. Which note is one and one half steps lower than F? _____
18. Which note is one and one half steps lower than C? _____
19. Which note is two and one half steps higher than C? _____
20. Which note is two and one half steps higher than G? _____

21. Which note is two and one half steps higher than B? _____
22. Which note is two and one half steps higher than E? _____
23. Which note is two and one half steps lower than F? _____
24. Which notes is two and one half steps lower than C? _____
25. Which note is two and one half steps lower than E? _____
26. Which note is two and one half steps lower than A? _____

ANSWER TRUE OR FALSE

1.	The 3rd and 4th notes of the C major scale are one half step apart.	True	False
2.	The 7th and 8th notes of the C major scale are one half step apart.	True	False
3.	The 4th and 5th notes of the C major scale are one half step apart.	True	False
4.	The 6th and 7th notes of the C major scale are one step apart.	True	False
5.	The 2nd and 3rd notes of the C major scale are one half step apart.	True	False
6.	The 1st and 2nd notes of the C major scale are one step apart.	True	False
7.	The 5th and 6th notes of the C major scale are one half step apart.	True	False

STEPPING STONE NO. 2

EIGHT MORE STEPPING STONES TO GO

Chords are derived from scales. We will proceed to construct chords that have "C" as their name. Examples of such chords are C major, C minor, C augmented, C diminished, C7, C9, etc.

The same as a chemist must make use of formulas to produce various chemicals, the musician must use formulas to derive various chords. The musical formulas are quite simple and should cause the student no trouble whatsoever.

The formula for a major chord is the numbers 1 and 3 and 5. This means that if we were to take the first, third, and fifth notes of the C major scale, we will have derived the notes in the C major chord.

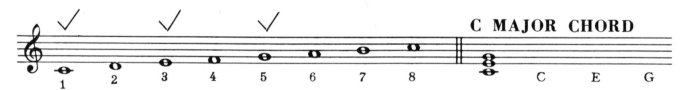

The formula for a minor chord is the numbers 1 and flatted 3, and 5. This means that if we were to take the first, flatted third, and fifth notes of the C major scale we will have derived the notes in the C minor chord.

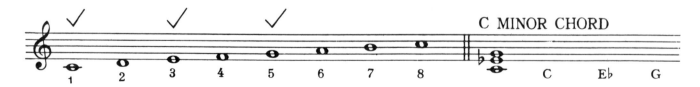

6

The formula for an augmented chord is the numbers 1 and 3, and sharped 5. This means that if we were to take the first, third, and sharped fifth notes of the C major scale we will have derived the notes in the C augmented chord.

The formula for the diminished 7 chord is the numbers 1 and flatted 3, and flatted 5, and double-flatted 7. A double-flatted note is one which is lowered two half steps (one full step). This means that if we were to take the first, flatted third, flatted fifth, and double-flatted seventh notes of the C major scale, we will have derived the notes in the C diminished 7 chord.

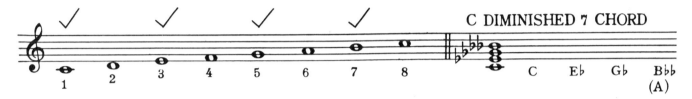

By knowing the formulas for the various chords, the student may use the C major scale to derive any C-type chord desired.

In order to derive 9th, 11th, or 13th-type chords, the C scale is written to encompass two octaves.

In actual practice, a major 6th chord is referred to as a 6th chord. A dominant 9th is referred to as a 9th chord. A dominant 7th is referred to as a 7th chord. A 13th chord is sometimes referred to as a 7 add 6 chord or a 9 add 6 chord.

ASSIGNMENT

Memorize all the formulas given below and then fill in the answers on the following page by deriving the required chords.

Major	1	3	5			
Minor	1	♭3	5			
Augmented	1	3	♯5			
Diminished	1	♭3	♭5			
Major 6	1	3	5	6		
Minor 6	1	♭3	5	6		
Dominant 7	1	3	5	♭7		
Major 7	1	3	5	7		
Minor 7	1	♭3	5	♭7		
Diminished 7 . .	1	♭3	♭5	♭♭7		

Augmented 7 . .	1	3	♯5	♭7		
7 flat 9	1	3	5	♭7	♭9	
7 sharp 9	1	3	5	♭7	♯9	
Dominant 9 . . .	1	3	5	♭7	9	
Major 9	1	3	5	7	9	
Minor 9	1	♭3	5	♭7	9	
Augmented 9 . .	1	3	♯5	♭7	9	
Diminished 9 . .	1	♭3	♭5	♭♭7	9	
13th	1	3	5	♭7	9	13
Augmented 11 .	1	3	5	♭7	9	♯11

STEPPING STONE NO. 3

SEVEN MORE STEPPING STONES TO GO

We have ascertained that the notes E and F, and the notes B and C are one half step apart. We have also found that in the C major scale, the third and fourth notes and the seventh and eighth notes are one half step apart, and that all the other adjacent notes are one step apart.

If all music were written in the key of C, we would now possess all the information necessary to commence playing jazz. However, because there are keys other than C major to consider, we will endeavor to familiarize ourselves with all the scales and the construction of chords from these scales.

Some years ago there was a well-known popular song which enjoyed fairly large record and sheet music sales, though the melody was simply an ascending and then descending C major scale:

Let us imagine that on the day of recording this song, the vocalist discovered that the lowest note possible for her to sing was a D, and that no matter how hard she tried she could not get her voice down to C, which is the first note of the song. Does this mean that our vocalist friend must give up the record session as a lost cause? Fortunately, the answer is no.

It would appear that the singer may start on the note D

and proceed through the musical alphabet until D   reappears.

However, since a D major scale is to be sung in place of the C major scale, the half steps and whole steps in the D major scale must be located similarly as the half steps and whole steps in the C major scale.

The vocalist must sing the D major scale in such a manner that, although it is one tone higher than the C major scale, it is *relatively* the same as the C major scale. Therefore, the first note is now D

and the scale will progress in the order of whole step, whole step, half step, whole step, whole step, whole step, half step, or exactly in the same manner as the C major scale.

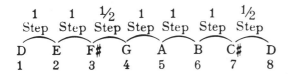

You will notice that in order to make the half steps appear between 3 and 4 and between 7 and 8, and to make the whole steps appear between 1 and 2; 2 and 3; 4 and 5; 5 and 6; 6 and 7; it was necessary to use sharps on the third and seventh notes of the scale.

Let us attempt to construct a G major scale. We will first write the note G and then proceed through the musical alphabet until G reappears.

G   A   B   C   D   E   F   G

Number the notes, one through eight.

G   A   B   C   D   E   F   G
1   2   3   4   5   6   7   8

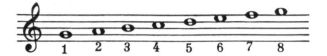

We now will draw connecting lines between the third and fourth notes and the seventh and eighth notes to remind us that these notes are one half step apart.

G   A   B   C   D   E   F   G
1   2   3   4   5   6   7   8

Now we will construct our scale.

1 to 2 should be one step apart.

   G to A are one step apart.

2 to 3 should be one step apart.

   A to B are one step apart.

3 to 4 should be one half step apart.

   B to C are one half step apart.

4 to 5 should be one step apart.

   C to D are one step apart.

5 to 6 should be one step apart.

   D to E are one step apart.

6 to 7 should be one step apart.

   E to F *are not one step apart.*

E to F are only one half step apart. In order to make these two notes one step apart, we must sharp the F. We could flat the E and produce the desired whole step between 6 and 7; however, by so doing, we would be creating one half step between 5 and 6, which obviously could be incorrect. 7 to 8 should be one half step apart.

   F♯ to G are one half step apart.

G   A   B   C   D   E   F♯ G
1   2   3   4   5   6   7   8

The G major scale contains one sharp (F♯). Hence, when we play in the key of G major, all the F notes will be sharped.

When music is written in the key of G major, the sharp is placed at the beginning of the song, on the fifth line of the staff (which is F) instead of being placed in front of every F note:

When we see the F♯ we know that the music is written in the key of G major. We are immediately informed of the key in which the music is written without having to look further through the music.

Those sharps or flats (or lack of them in the key of C major) which appear at the beginning of a selection are called the *key signature*. The key signature appears between the treble clef sign and the time signature, which is present in all guitar music:

At times we will come across a piece of music which contains a sharp or flat in its context which does not appear in the key signature. Because this is an exception to the rule and because this sharp or flat is a harmonic "accident," this sharp or flat is called an *accidental.*

ASSIGNMENT

To become familiar with the various scales, the student should construct all the 15 major scales on a sheet of manuscript paper and then check the results with the 15 scales given below. The scales should be written over and over until scale construction is possible with very little effort on the part of the student.

The major scales to be constructed are as follows:

C Major	F Major
G Major	B♭ Major
D Major	E♭ Major
A Major	A♭ Major
E Major	D♭ Major
B Major	G♭ Major
F♯ Major	C♭ Major
C♯ Major	

C Major   **C D E F G A B C**

G Major   **G A B C D E F♯ G**

D Major	D	E	F#	G	A	B	C#	D
A Major	A	B	C#	D	E	F#	G#	A
E Major	E	F#	G#	A	B	C#	D#	E
B Major	B	C#	D#	E	F#	G#	A#	B
F# Major	F#	G#	A#	B	C#	D#	E#	F#
C# Major	C#	D#	E#	F#	G#	A#	B#	C#
F Major	F	G	A	B♭	C	D	E	F
B♭ Major	B♭	C	D	E♭	F	G	A	B♭
E♭ Major	E♭	F	G	A♭	B♭	C	D	E♭
A♭ Major	A♭	B♭	C	D♭	E♭	F	G	A♭
D♭ Major	D♭	E♭	F	G♭	A♭	B♭	C	D♭
G♭ Major	G♭	A♭	B♭	C♭	D♭	E♭	F	G♭
C♭ Major	C♭	D♭	E♭	F♭	G♭	A♭	B♭	C♭

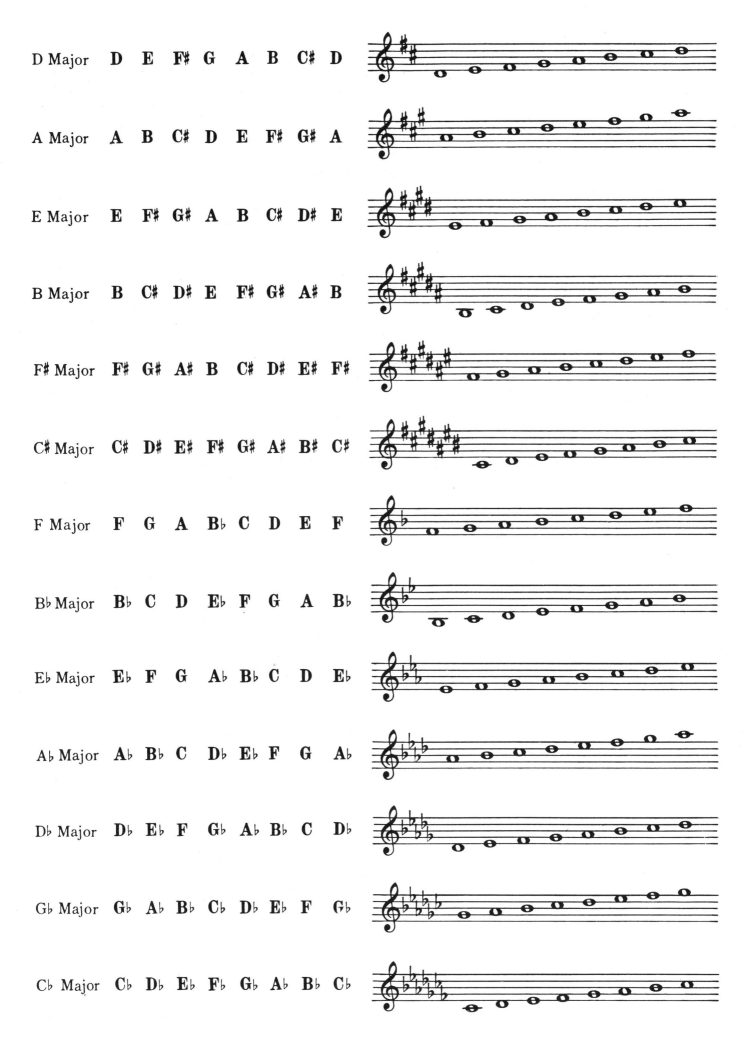

STEPPING STONE NO. 4

SIX MORE STEPPING STONES TO GO

When a scale contains 1 sharp, the sharped note is F.

When a scale contains 2 sharps, the sharped notes are F and C.

When a scale contains 3 sharps, the sharped notes are F, C, G.

When a scale contains 4 sharps, the sharped notes are F, C, G, D.

When a scale contains 5 sharps, the sharped notes are F, C, G, D, A.

When a scale contains 6 sharps, the sharped notes are F, C, G, D, A, E.

When a scale contains 7 sharps, the sharped notes are F, C, G, D, A, E, B.

By memorizing the order in which the sharps appear (F, C, G, D, A, E, B) the student can quickly determine which notes are sharped in each sharped scale.

The order in which the flats appear is exactly the reverse of the sharps. When a scale contains only one flat, the flatted note is B. When a scale contains two flats, the flatted notes are B and E, etc.

Sharps in Order: F C G D A E B

Flats in Order: B E A D G C F

When a scale contains 1 sharp, the scale is a G major scale.

When a scale contains 2 sharps, the scale is a D major scale.

When a scale contains 3 sharps, the scale is an A major scale.

When a scale contains 4 sharps, the scale is an E major scale.

When a scale contains 5 sharps, the scale is a B major scale.

When a scale contains 6 sharps, the scale is an F♯ major scale.

When a scale contains 7 sharps, the scale is a C♯ major scale.

The sharped scales, in order of the amount of sharps they contain, are:

G   D   A   E   B   F♯   C♯

The flatted scales, in order of the amount of flats they contain, are:

F   B♭   E♭   A♭   D♭   G♭   C♭

ASSIGNMENT

How many sharps are in the G scale?	_____	Which are they?	_____
How many flats are in the F scale?	_____	Which are they?	_____
How many flats are in the E♭ scale?	_____	Which are they?	_____
How many sharps are in the D scale?	_____	Which are they?	_____
How many sharps are in the E scale?	_____	Which are they?	_____
How many flats are in the B♭ scale?	_____	Which are they?	_____
How many sharps are in the A scale?	_____	Which are they?	_____
How many sharps are in the B scale?	_____	Which are they?	_____
How many sharps are in the C♯ scale?	_____	Which are they?	_____
How many flats are in the A♭ scale?	_____	Which are they?	_____
How many sharps are in the F♯ scale?	_____	Which are they?	_____
How many flats are in the G♭ scale?	_____	Which are they?	_____
How many flats are in the D♭ scale?	_____	Which are they?	_____
How many flats are in the C♭ scale?	_____	Which are they?	_____

In the key of 1 sharp, which note is sharped? _____

In the key of 1 flat, which notes is flatted? _____

In the key of 2 sharps, which notes are sharped? _____

In the key of 2 flats, which notes are flatted? _____

In the key of 3 sharps, which notes are sharped? _____

In the key of 3 flats, which notes are flatted? _____

In the key of 4 sharps, which notes are sharped? _____

In the key of 4 flats, which notes are flatted? _____

In the key of 5 sharps, which notes are sharped? _____

In the key of 5 flats, which notes are flatted? _____

In the key of 6 sharps, which notes are sharped? _____

In the key of 6 flats, which notes are flatted? _____

In the key of 7 sharps, which notes are sharped? _____

In the key of 7 flats, which notes are flatted? _____

STEPPING STONE NO. 5

FIVE MORE STEPPING STONES TO GO

In order to derive chords from the various constructed scales, we will follow the same procedure outlined in Stepping Stone No. 2. Major chord is 1, 3, 5. Minor chord is 1, flat 3, 5, etc. When deriving a D-type chord, use the D major scale. When deriving a B-type chord, use the B major scale. When deriving an E flat-type chord, use the E flat major scale.

ASSIGNMENT

Below are all 15 scales with the derived major, minor, augmented, diminished 7, and dominant 7 chords. The student should write out all the scales and then derive the aforementioned chords. The answers should be checked against those given below.

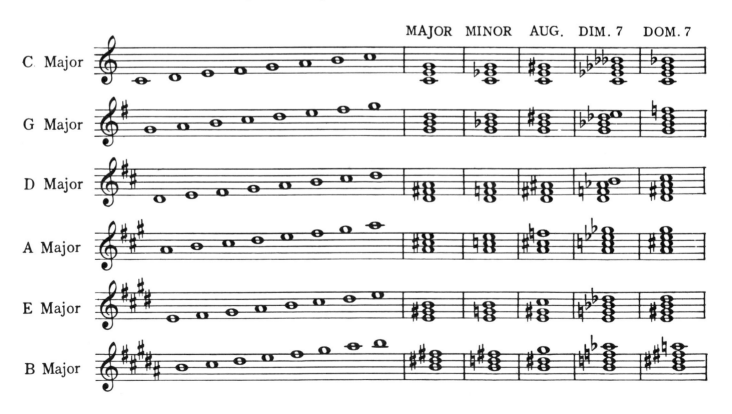

14

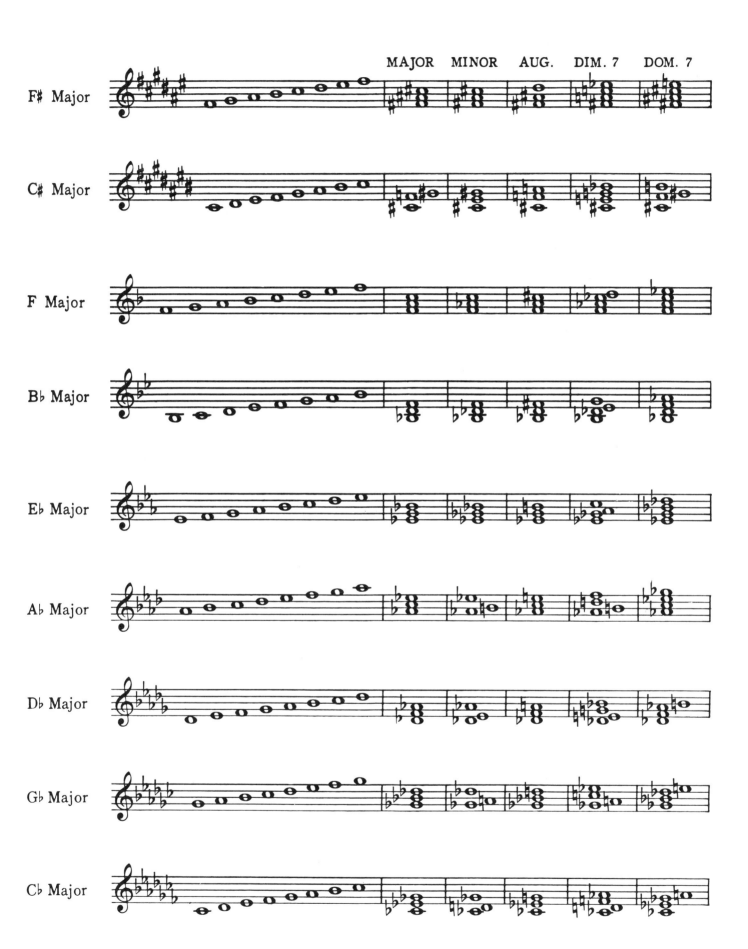

STEPPING STONE NO. 6

FOUR MORE STEPPING STONES TO GO

The C major scale is composed of the notes C, D, E, F, G, A, B, C.

The formulas for deriving a major chord is 1, 3, 5. The C major chord contains the notes C, E, G.

When a chord contains three *different* notes, the chord is called a *triad.* The C major chord, for example, may contain many C's, many E's, many G's. However, since there are only *three different* notes, the chord is still a triad.

The letter name of a chord is called the *root.* The root of a G minor chord is G. The root of a D7 chord is D. The root of a B major chord is B. The root of an E flat 6 chord is E flat.

The major chord contains a root, third, and fifth. When the root is the lowest note, the chord is said to be in *root position.*

     C major chord in root position.

When the "third" of the chord is the lowest note, the chord is in the first inversion.

     C major chord in first inversion.

When the "fifth" of the chord is the lowest note, the chord is in the second inversion.

     C major chord in second inversion.

Any chord may be inverted. When a chord is inverted, it retains its root name.

Example: C   E   G   form a C major chord

E   G   C   form a C major chord

G   C   E   form a C major chord

ASSIGNMENT

Construct all 15 major scales and derive all major and minor chords. Write all major and minor chords in root position, first inversion, and second inversion.

16

STEPPING STONE NO. 7

THREE MORE STEPPING STONES TO GO

Up to this point we have referred to the notes of the scale by letter name or by number. Another manner of designating the scale notes is by *technical name.*

1st note of the scale	TONIC	5th note of the scale	DOMINANT
2nd note of the scale	SUPERTONIC	6th note of the scale	SUBMEDIANT
3rd note of the scale	MEDIANT	7th notes of the scale	LEADING TONE
4th note of the scale	SUBDOMINANT	8th note of the scale	OCTAVE

C MAJOR SCALE

D MAJOR SCALE

ASSIGNMENT

The technical names for each degree of the scale of all scales should be memorized. The student should also review all material covered up to this point.

STEPPING STONE NO. 8

TWO MORE STEPPING STONES TO GO

For the jazz musician, a knowledge of intervals is a necessity. An *interval* is the distance between two tones or the difference in pitch between two tones.

Intervals are referred to by numbers. Examples are 2nd, 3rd, 4th, 5th, 6th, 7th, octave for 8th, 9th, 10th, 11th, and 13th.

As we already know, the notes used in music are the same as the first seven letters of the alphabet.

A B C D E F G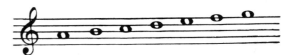

Any two notes (letters) which are next to each other form an interval of a second: A to B, B to C, C to D, D to E, E to F, F to G, G to A.

If the distance between notes includes three letters, then the interval is a third: A to C (ABC), B to D (BCD), C to E (CDE), D to F (DEF), E to G (EFG), F to A (FGA), G to B (GAB).

If the distance between notes includes four letters, then the interval is a fourth: A to D (ABCD), B to E (BCDE), C to F (CDEF), D to G (DEFG), E to A (EFGA), F to B (FGAB), G to C (GABC).

A seventh higher than D is C (DEFGABC). A sixth higher than B is G (BCDEFG). A ninth higher than F is G (FGABCDEFG).

17

Intervals may also be counted downward. A third lower than G is E (GFE). A fifth lower than F is B (FEDCB).

When the same note is played by two different instruments or when the same note is played on two different strings of the guitar, the interval is referred to as a *prime,* and the notes are said to be in *unison.*

In addition to the number name for intervals, there is also a type name.

C to D is an interval of a second. C sharp to D is an interval of a second. C to D sharp is an interval of a second. C to D flat is an interval of a second. As you can see, there are shortcomings to using only the interval number name. Below is a table of the type names of intervals. The student should study this table in order to become familiar with the various intervals.

C to D♭	Half step	Minor 2nd
C♯ to D	Half step	Minor 2nd
C to D	Whole step	Major 2nd
C to D♯	One and one half steps	Augmented 2nd
C to E♭	One and one half steps	Minor 3rd
C to E	Two steps	Major 3rd
C to F	Two and one half steps	Perfect 4th
C to F♯	Three steps	Augmented 4th
C to G♭	Three steps	Diminished 5th
C to G	Three and one half steps	Perfect 5th
C to G♯	Four steps	Augmented 5th
C♯ to A	Four steps	Minor 6th
C to A♭	Four steps	Minor 6th
C to A	Four and one half steps	Major 6th
C to A♯	Five steps	Augmented 6th
C♯ to B♭	Four and one half steps	Diminished 7th
C to B♭	Five steps	Minor 7th
C to B	Five and one half steps	Major 7th
C to C	Six steps	Perfect octave

When a major interval is increased one half step, it becomes augmented.

When a major interval is decreased one half step, it becomes minor.

When a Perfect interval is increased one half step, it becomes augmented.

When a Perfect interval is decreased one half step, it becomes diminished.

When a minor interval is decreased one half step, it becomes diminished.

When a diminished interval is decreased one half step, it becomes double diminished.

ASSIGNMENT

Which note is a minor second higher than D? _____

Which note is a major second higher than F? _____

Which note is a minor third higher than G? _____

Which note is a major third higher than G? _____

Which note is a perfect fourth higher than A? _____

Which note is an augmented fourth higher than A? _____

Which note is a perfect fifth higher than G? _____

Which note is an augmented fifth higher than G? _____

Which note is a diminished fifth higher than G? _____

Which note is a major sixth higher than C? _____

Which note is a minor sixth higher than C? _____

Which note is a minor seventh higher than D? _____

Which note is a major seventh higher than D? _____

Which note is an octave higher than B? _____

Which note is a major second higher than D? _____

Which note is a major second higher than A? _____

Which note is a minor second higher than A? _____

Which note is a major second higher than B? _____

Which note is a minor second higher than B? _____

Which note is a major second higher than E? _____

Which note is a minor second higher than E? _____

Which note is a major third higher than C? _____

Which note is a minor third higher than C? _____

Which note is a major third higher than D? _____

Which note is a minor third higher than D? _____

Which note is a major third higher than E? _____

Which note is a minor third higher than E? _____

Which note is a perfect fourth higher than B? _____

Which note is a perfect fourth higher than C? _____

Which note is a perfect fourth higher than G? _____

Which note is a perfect fifth higher than A? _____

Which note is a perfect fifth higher than C? _____

Which note is a perfect fifth higher than B? _____

Which note is a major sixth higher than D? _____

STEPPING STONE NO. 9
ONE MORE STEPPING STONE TO GO

The C major chord contains the notes	C	E	G
The D major chord contains the notes	D	F♯	A
The E major chord contains the notes	E	G♯	B
The F major chord contains the notes	F	A	C
The G major chord contains the notes	G	B	D
The A major chord contains the notes	A	C♯	E
The B major chord contains the notes	B	D♯	F♯

The notes in all of the above major chords should be memorized. When this is accomplished, it is a simple matter to raise or lower by one half step the notes in the memorized chords to determine the sharp or flat major chords.

For example, the F major chord contains the notes F and A and C. The F♯ major chord would contain the notes F♯ and A♯ and C♯. The G major chord contains the notes G and B and D. The G♭ major chord would contain the notes G♭ and B♭ and D♭.

When the notes in the major chords are memorized, it is equally easy to derive the major 7 chord by adding to the major chord a note which is one half step lower than the root. For example, the F major chord contains the notes F and A and C. The F major 7 chord contains the notes F and A and C and E. The G major chord contains G and B and D. The G major 7 chord contains G and B and D and F♯.

To derive the dominant 7 chord, add to the major chord a note which is one step lower than the root. For example, the C major chord contains the notes C and E and G. The C7 chord contains the notes C and E and G and B♭. The D major chord is comprised of the notes D and F♯ and A. The D7 chord is made up of D and F♯ and A and C.

To derive the major 9 chord, add to the major 7 chord a note which is one step higher than the root. For example, the C major 7 chord contains the notes C and E and G and B. The C major 9 chord contains the notes C and E and G and B and D. The D major 7 chord contains the notes D and F♯ and A and C♯. The D major 9 chord contains the notes D and F♯ and A and C♯ and E.

To derive the dominant 9 chord, add to the dominant 7 chord a note which is one step higher than the root. For example, G7 contains the notes G and B and D and F. The G9 chord contains the notes G and B and D and F and A. The F7 chord contains the notes F and A and C and E♭. The F9 chord contains the notes F and A and C and E♭ and G.

To derive the major 6 chord, add to the major chord a note which is one step higher than the fifth. For example, C major contains the notes C and E and G. The C6 chord contains the notes C and E and G and A. The D major chord contains the notes D and F♯ and A. The D6 chord contains the notes D and F♯ and A and B.

20

To derive the minor 7 chord, lower the third of the dominant 7 chord one half step. For example, C7 contains the notes C and E and G and B♭. The C minor 7 contains the notes C and E♭ and G and B♭. The D7 contains D and F♯ and A and C. The D minor 7 contains the notes D and F and A and C.

To derive the minor 6 chord, lower the third of the major 6 chord one half step. For example, C6 contains the notes C and E and G and A. The C minor 6 contains the notes C and E♭ and G and A. The D6 chord contains the notes D and F♯ and A and B. The D minor 6 chord contains the notes D and F and A and B.

ASSIGNMENT

Which notes form the E major chord?   _____

Which notes form the A major 7 chord?   _____

Which notes form the D6 chord?   _____

Which notes form the G7 chord?   _____

Which notes form the C9 chord?   _____

Which notes form the F minor 6 chord?   _____

Which notes form the B♭ major chord?   _____

Which notes form the E♭ minor chord?   _____

Which notes form the A♭ minor 7 chord?   _____

Which notes form the D♭7 chord?   _____

Which notes form the G♭6 chord?   _____

Which notes form the B major 7 chord?   _____

Which notes form the E minor 6 chord?   _____

Which notes form the A minor 6 chord?   _____

Which notes form the D7 chord?   _____

Which notes form the G minor chord?   _____

Which notes form the C7 chord?   _____

Which notes form the F6 chord?   _____

Which notes form the B♭7 chord?   _____

Which notes form the E♭9 chord?   _____

Which notes form the A♭ major 9 chord?   _____

Which notes form the D♭ minor 9 chord?   _____

Which notes form the G♭ minor chord?   _____

STEPPING STONE NO. 10

THE LAST STEPPING STONE

In applying theory to the study of jazz, the student will discover that a great deal of freedom is permissible in playing a jazz solo.

It was mentioned earlier that chords are based upon scales and that jazz is based upon chords. There are definite notes in each chord. However, when playing a jazz solo the musician is permitted the liberty of adding or omitting notes from the given chord.

One manner of "adding" notes to the given chord is by the use of *passing tones*. A passing tone is a note (not contained within the chord) which may be played when passing from one chord note to another chord note. It is acceptable for the jazz musician to use more than one passing tone as long as the chord sound is established. Passing tones will be dealt with quite thoroughly later on in this volume.

Substitution is another manner in which "out-of-the-chord notes" may be used during a jazz solo. In many instances the chords which appear on the sheet for the jazz tune are too empty. It is permissible for the jazz musician to substitute another chord for the original chord for the purpose of making the jazz chorus richer in sound. The replacement of a written chord by another chord (unwritten) is known as chord substitution.

Chord substitution will be discussed in great detail in Part Two. Below are some examples of chord substitution.

Chord That Appears on the Music	Chord(s) Which May Be Substituted for the Given Chord
Major	Major 6 or major 7 or major 9
Minor	Minor 6 or minor 7 or minor aug. or minor with major 7
Dominant 7	9th or 13th or aug. 7 or aug. 9 or 7($\flat$5)

At times a chord called a *major suspended* or a *dominant 7 suspended* may appear in the music. A suspended chord is one in which the third of the chord has been raised one half step higher, to a fourth. For example, C major contains C and E and G. The C suspended chord contains C and F and G. The G7 chord contains the notes G and B and D and F. The G7 sus. chord contains the notes G and C and D and F.

We have at this point completed the music theory necessary to start our lessons on jazz solo playing. It is not this writer's intent to lead the student to believe that all aspects of music theory have been explained. For the student who wishes to delve more deeply into theory, there are many fine books on this subject. There also are courses given in theory in many of the music schools and studios throughout the nation.

ASSIGNMENT

Thoroughly review everything covered up to this point.

Below is an easy reference chord chart which the student may use to look up sharps, flats, key signatures, chord spellings, and chord derivations.

CHORD CHART

KEY	MAJOR	MINOR	AUG.	DIM.	DOM. 7th	MAJ. 7th	MIN. 7th	MAJ. 6th	MIN. 6th
KEY OF C MAJOR (NO #'s — NO b's)	CEG	CEbG	CEG#	CEbGbA	CEGBb	CEGB	CEbGBb	CEGA	CEbGA
KEY OF G MAJOR F#	GBD	GBbD	GBD#	GBbDbE	GBDF	GBDF#	GBbDF	GBDE	GBbDE
KEY OF D MAJOR F# - C#	DF#A	DFA	DF#A#	DFAbB	DF#AC	DF#AC#	DFAC	DF#AB	DFAB
KEY OF A MAJOR F# - C# - G#	AC#E	ACE	AC#F	ACEbGb	AC#EG	AC#EG#	ACEG	AC#EF#	ACEF#
KEY OF E MAJOR F# - C# - G# - D#	EG#B	EGB	EG#C	EGBbDb	EG#BD	EG#BD#	EGBD	EG#BC#	EGBC#
KEY OF B MAJOR F# - C# - G# - D# - A#	BD#F#	BDF#	BD#G	BDFAb	BD#F#A	BD#F#A#	BDF#A	BD#F#G#	BDF#G#
KEY OF F# MAJOR F# - C# - G# - D# - A# - E#	F#A#C#	F#AC#	F#A#D	F#ACD#	F#A#C#E	F#A#C#E#	F#AC#E	F#A#C#D#	F#AC#D#
KEY OF C# MAJOR F# - C# - G# - D# - A# - E# - B#	C#E#G#	C#EG#	C#E#A	C#EGA#	C#E#G#B	C#E#G#B#	C#EG#B	C#E#G#A#	C#EG#A#
KEY OF F MAJOR Bb	FAC	FAbC	FAC#	FAbBD	FACEb	FACE	FAbCEb	FACD	FAbCD
KEY OF Bb MAJOR Bb - Eb	BbDF	BbDbF	BbDF#	BbDbEG	BbDFAb	BbDFA	BbDbFAb	BbDFG	BbDbFG
KEY OF Eb MAJOR Bb - Eb - Ab	EbGBb	EbGbBb	EbGB	EbGbAC	EbGBbDb	EbGBbD	EbGbBbDb	EbGBbC	EbGbBbC
KEY OF Ab MAJOR Bb - Eb - Ab - Db	AbCEb	AbBEb	AbCE	AbBDF	AbCEbGb	AbCEbG	AbCbEbGb	AbCEbF	AbBEbF
KEY OF Db MAJOR Bb - Eb - Ab - Db - Gb	DbFAb	DbEAb	DbFA	DbEGBb	DbFAbB	DbFAbC	DbEAbB	DbFAbBb	DbEAbBb
KEY OF Gb MAJOR Bb - Eb - Ab - Db - Gb - Cb	GbBbDb	GbADb	GbBbD	GbACEb	GbBbDbFb	GbBbDbF	GbADbE	GbBbDbEb	GbADbEb
KEY OF Cb MAJOR Bb - Eb - Ab - Db - Gb - Cb - Fb	CbEbGb	CbDGb	CbEbG	CbDFAb	CbEbGbA	CbEbGbBb	CbDGbA	CbEbGbAb	CbDGbAb

CHORD DERIVATIONS

MAJOR: 1—3—5

MINOR: 1—b3—5

AUGMENTED: 1—3—#5

DIMINISHED: 1—b3—b5—bb7

DOMINANT 7TH: 1—3—5—b7

MAJOR 7TH: 1—3—5—7

MINOR 7TH: 1—b3—5—b7

MAJOR 6TH: 1—3—5—6

MINOR 6TH: 1—b3—5—6

AUGMENTED 7TH: 1—3—#5—b7

JAZZ SOLO COURSE
LESSON 1

JAZZ IS A MUSICAL LINE which, when played in place of the melody (song), will blend with the chord accompaniment that is intended for the song melody.

The chord accompaniment may be supplied by another guitar, a piano, any chordal instrument, or an orchestra. In the case of an orchestra, chord accompaniment is supplied by the various orchestral instruments providing the different notes necessary to form chords. If one trumpet plays the note C, a second trumpet plays the note E, a third trumpet plays the note G, then the resultant chord produced by the three trumpets playing simultaneously would be a C major chord.

Because a jazz chorus will not sound like the melody of the song, it is customary for the melody to be played during the first chorus. For this reason, the listener or dancer, without realizing why, will retain the song melody in his or her mind during the second and subsequent choruses while the jazz choruses are being played.

Many jazz enthusiasts are of the impression that they can hear the melody being played during the jazz chorus. The fallacy of this belief may be proven by playing a recording of a well-known song for a friend. Start the record in the middle, during the jazz chorus. If your friend is not a musician and has not heard the recording before, it is doubtful that he or she will be able to determine the melody by listening to the jazz chorus.

It is only after listening to the first chorus of melody that the jazz chorus will sound like the melody with a few variations added.

In many orchestras the leaders frown upon the playing of jazz choruses. Some musicians please the leader and at the same time avoid the monotony of repeating the melody by mixing jazz with the melody. This may be done by playing a few measures of the melody and then a few bars of jazz.

Jazz is a musical line which is built upon the same chords as the melody.

On the following page is the melody to "A Hunting We Will Go." The accompaniment chords are indicated above the melody. Following this is a jazz chorus. Notice that the accompaniment chords are the same for the melody and the jazz chorus.

There are only two accompaniment chords employed in "A Hunting We Will Go." The chords are C major (CEG) and G7 (GBDF).

With the exception of the fifth measure, all the notes played in the jazz chorus during the C major accompaniment chord consist only of the notes C, E, and G.

The notes played during the G7 accompaniment chord (last two beats of the seventh measure) consist of the notes GBDF.

It was explained earlier that substitution chords may be used in place of the given chord. In the fifth measure, C6 (CEGA) was substituted for C major.

Because we are dealing with jazz in its most elementary form, the jazz choruses used at this time will tend to sound elementary in their construction.

Study the jazz chorus carefully so that the foregoing is thoroughly understood.

Below is another example of a jazz chorus on "A Hunting We Will Go." Though there is a difference in style between the two jazz choruses, both choruses are comprised of the notes contained in the accompaniment chords.

It is permissible for the chord notes to be "mixed" in any order and for their time values to be changed.

Smearing a note is achieved by the left-hand finger pulling the depressed note for the purpose of raising the pitch. The pulled note is then allowed to return to its normal position and normal pitch.

ASSIGNMENT

To become familiar with the ingredients in a jazz chorus, the student should write five jazz choruses for "A Hunting We Will Go."

The student should not be concerned at this time with the sound of the jazz chorus as much as with an understanding of the construction of the chorus. The chord notes may be mixed in any order and given any time values which the student may desire.

A Hunting We Will Go

LESSON 2

The following is another example of a jazz chorus. The melody is "Merrily We Roll Along." The student should study and analyze the jazz chorus carefully. At this time, an understanding of jazz is of more importance than an attempt to play jazz.

Merrily We Roll Along

The student will observe that only two chords were needed for "Merrily We Roll Along." Notes used in the jazz chorus other than chordal notes were either passing tones or the result of chord substitution or both.

Although the jazz choruses presented thus far are technically correct, they would tend to sound overly basic because we are using very few passing tones or chord substitutions. (Chord substitutions will be covered in great detail in Part Two.)

The student may test his or her ability to write jazz choruses by having another guitarist play the accompaniment chords while the student plays the jazz choruses written out in Lesson 1.

ASSIGNMENT

The student should write five jazz choruses for "Merrily We Roll Along." The student may take advantage of chord substitution. For the C major chord, the C major 6, C major 7, or C major 9 may be substituted. The chord notes may be mixed in any order and given any time values which the student desires.

Merrily We Roll Along

LESSON 3

For the most part, jazz is comprised of runs and/or riffs. A run is a flowing succession of notes. A riff is a repetitive theme played over and over throughout a portion or an entire jazz chorus.

EXAMPLE RUN: EXAMPLE RIFF:

Below is a chord progression which is used for the accompaniment of many songs.

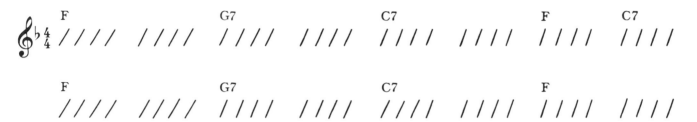

Below is a jazz chorus which may be played against the chord progression.

Notice that the first eight measures are composed of runs. The last eight measures are a riff.

Here is another example of a jazz chorus built upon the same chord progression.

29

ASSIGNMENT

The student should write ten different jazz choruses based upon the previous chord progression. The student may mix the chord notes in any manner desired. The time values of the notes are left to the discretion of the student. Chord substitutions may be used.

After the ten jazz choruses have been written, the student should play the choruses. If possible, another guitar player should play the accompaniment chords while the student plays the written jazz choruses.

LESSON 4

When playing jazz with a group or orchestra, the musician is not afforded the opportunity to carefully figure out each note of the jazz chorus while playing. Does this mean that the jazz soloist thinks strictly in terms of the notes in the chord accompaniment, and then trusts to luck that the sequence and time patterns of the notes played will provide an interesting jazz chorus? No, it does not.

The first approach to playing jazz is figuring out various runs and riffs which will fit the necessary chords. Those runs and riffs and ideas which seem most pleasing are memorized. Through years of playing, the memorized ideas change and finally are used as a skeleton structure for new ideas, new runs, new riffs. When experienced jazz artists are called upon to "take off" on an F major chord, for example, they do not say to themselves, "How can I mix the F and A and C notes to produce a good jazz sound?" Instead they think in terms of that which they *know* (as a result of past experience) will fit in with the accompaniment chord. They also listen very carefully to the background being played behind them to inspire them to greater heights in building up the predetermined jazz skeleton structure.

Because all jazz musicians possess these basic skeleton outlines upon which they base their jazz, they always retain, even after many years of playing, portions of their ideas which were conceived when their jazz musicianship was in the embryonic stage. It is because of this that each jazz musician will tend to have his or her own style.

To use an analogy, we may say that this lesson is devoted to the hanging of wires upon which to build the jazz skeleton structure.

Here is a 2-measure F7 run which the student should memorize. It is extremely important that the run be played in the first position and that the fingerings be played *exactly as written.*

1st POSITION

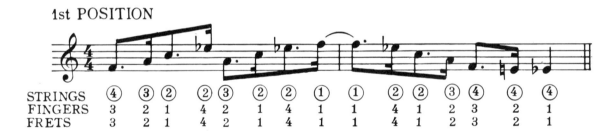

STRINGS	④	③ ②	② ③	②	②	①	①	②	②	③	④	④	④
FINGERS	3	2 1	4 2	1	4	1	1	4	1	2	3	2	1
FRETS	3	2 1	4 2	1	4	1	1	4	1	2	3	2	1

When the F7 run is memorized so thoroughly that the guitarist can play it as though it were second nature, the left hand should be moved up to the third position. (The word "position" means the fret upon which the first finger is pressing. "Third position" would mean that the first finger plays the notes on the third fret, the second finger plays the notes on the fourth fret, the third finger plays the notes on the fifth fret, and the fourth finger plays the notes on the sixth fret.)

Because the same fingering and strings are now used in the third position as were used in the first position, the runs are *relatively* the same. The difference is that the F7 run is raised one tone (one step) in pitch. The run which was an F7 run in the first position is now a G7 run when played in the third position.

3rd POSITION

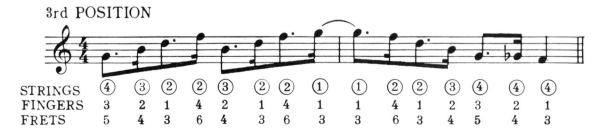

STRINGS	④	③	②	② ③	②	②	①	①	②	②	③	④	④	④
FINGERS	3	2	1	4 2	1	4	1	1	4	1	2	3	2	1
FRETS	5	4	3	6 4	3	6	3	3	6	3	4	5	4	3

By same token, the previous dominant 7 run fingering may be played on any position of the guitar fingerboard to produce dominant 7 runs of different root names.

The following are the root names of the given dominant 7 run, when played on the various positions of the guitar fingerboard. Memorize them thoroughly.

First position	F7	Seventh Position	B7
Second position	F♯7 or G♭7	Eighth position	C7
Third position	G7	Ninth position	C♯7 or D♭7
Fourth position	G♯7 or A♭7	Tenth position	D7
Fifth position	A7	Eleventh position	D♯7 or E♭7
Sixth position	A♯7 or B♭7	Twelfth position	E7

ASSIGNMENT

Play the following exercise, using the memorized dominant 7 run form.

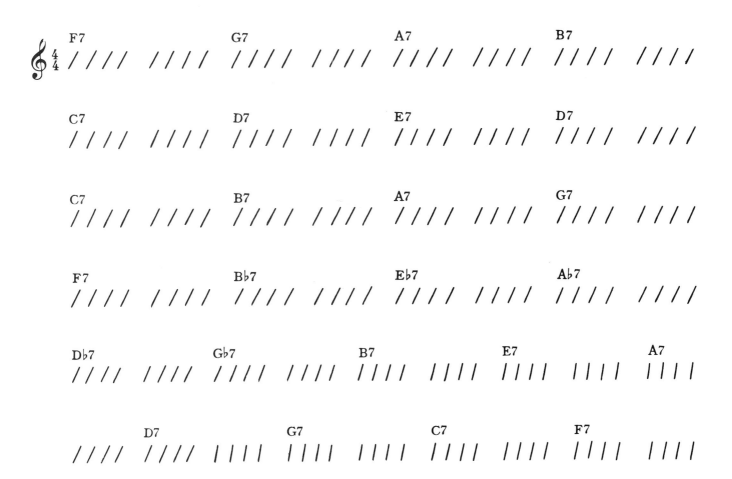

33

LESSON 5

As we have already learned, jazz solos are built upon chords. The following chord sequence is not uncommon.

G7   C7   F7   B♭7   E♭7   A♭

If we were to build a jazz chorus upon these chords using the dominant 7 form studied in Lesson 4, it would be necessary to play the G7 run in the third position, the C7 run in the eighth position, the F7 run in the first position, the B♭7 run in the sixth position, and the E♭7 run in the eleventh position.

It is evident that the position jumps would be awkward and that the repetition of the same run form would sound monotonous. Therefore, it is necessary to become familiar with another dominant 7 run form.

D7 RUN 2nd POSITION

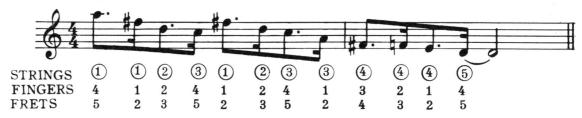

STRINGS	①	①	②	③	①	②	③	③	④	④	④	⑤
FINGERS	4	1	2	4	1	2	4	1	3	2	1	4
FRETS	5	2	3	5	2	3	5	2	4	3	2	5

The D7 run should be memorized. Strict attention should be paid to following the given strings, fingerings, and frets.

As indicated below, the new dominant 7 run form may be played on all the fingerboard positions. Memorize them thoroughly.

First position	C♯7 or D♭7
Second position	D7
Third position	D♯7 or E♭7
Fourth position	E7
Fifth position	F7
Sixth position	F♯7 or G♭7
Seventh position	G7
Eighth position	G♯7 or A♭7
Ninth position	A7
Tenth position	A♯7 or B♭7
Eleventh position	B7
Twelfth position	C7

ASSIGNMENT

Practice the following exercise, using the newly learned dominant 7 run form.

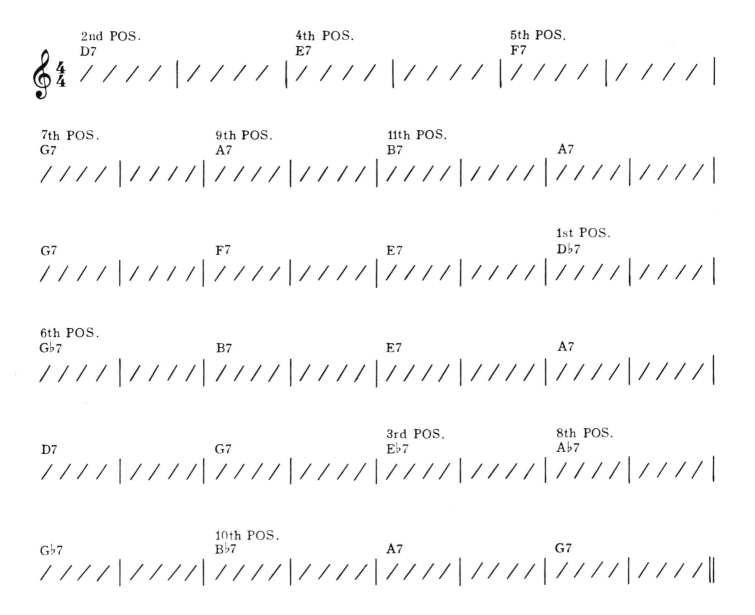

35

LESSON 6

The following exercise will give the student practice on both dominant 7 run forms. Observe the positions indicated above the chord symbols.

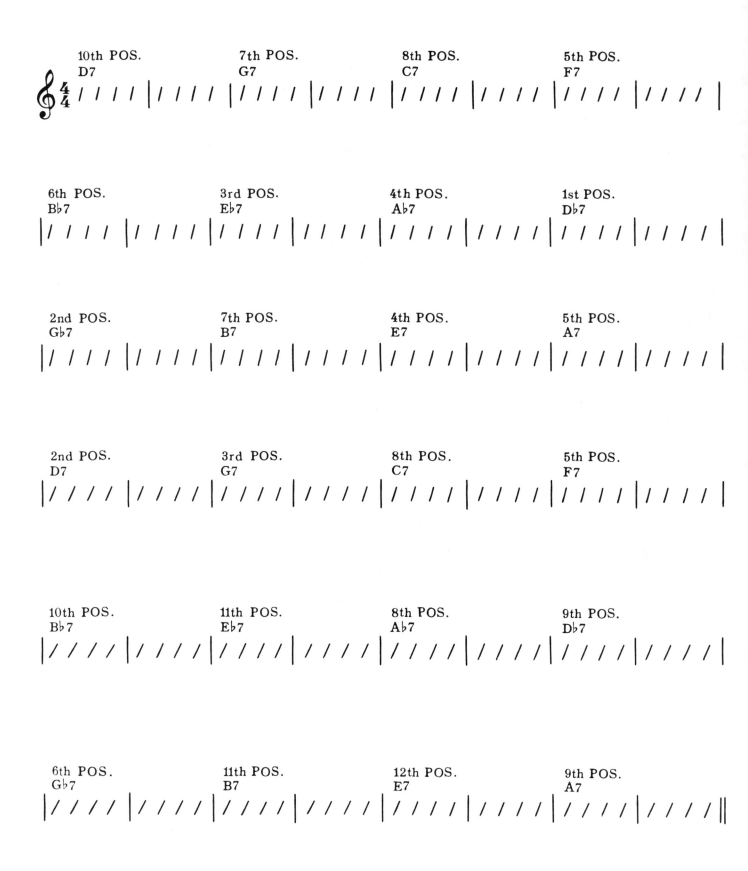

LESSON 7

Below is a major run form. When played in the first position, the run is an F major run. Memorize it, using the given strings, fingerings, and frets.

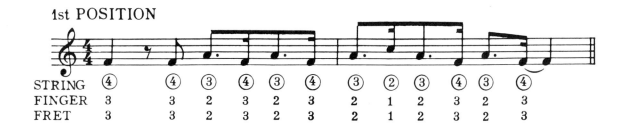

The following are the root names of the major run when played on the various positions of the fingerboard. Memorize them thoroughly.

First position	F major
Second position	F♯ or G♭ major
Third position	G major
Fourth position	G♯ or A♭ major
Fifth position	A major
Sixth position	A♯ or B♭ major
Seventh position	B major
Eighth position	C major
Ninth position	C♯ or D♭ major
Tenth position	D major
Eleventh position	D♯ or E♭ major
Twelfth position	E major

ASSIGNMENT

Practice the exercise, using the newly learned major run form.

37

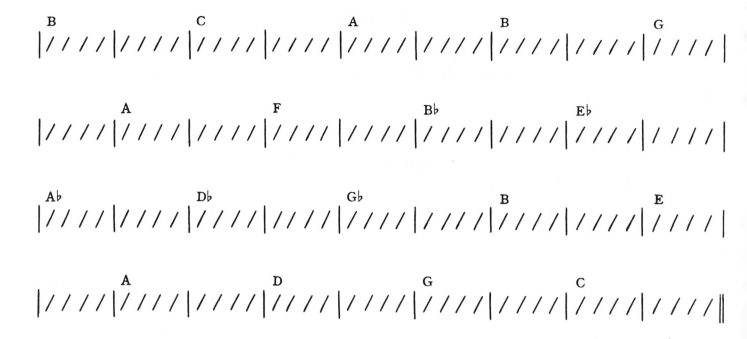

Below is a chord progression which will fit many standard tunes. The student should play a jazz chorus using the runs learned thus far. If possible, the chord accompaniment should be played by another guitarist while the jazz chorus is played by the student.

NOTE: When a chord appears for only one measure, the first measure of the memorized run should be used.

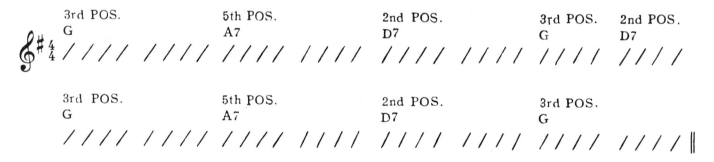

LESSON 8

It is advisable that the student review all material covered up to this point. It is also suggested that the student listen to as much jazz as possible. By listening to others play jazz, the student can analyze how experienced jazz artists "handle" the chords to produce interesting jazz choruses.

The following are two minor run forms. Memorize these two forms and then learn the names of these runs in all the positions.

First position	F minor	Seventh position	B minor
Second position	F♯ or G♭ minor	Eighth position	C minor
Third position	G minor	Ninth position	C♯ or D♭ minor
Fourth position	G♯ or A♭ minor	Tenth position	D minor
Fifth position	A minor	Eleventh position	D♯ or E♭ minor
Sixth position	A♯ or B♭ minor	Twelfth position	E minor

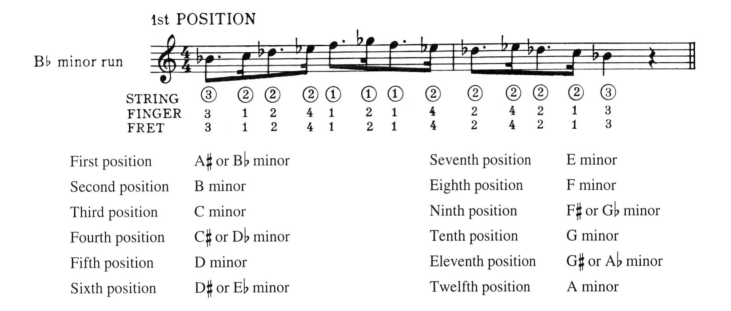

First position	A♯ or B♭ minor	Seventh position	E minor
Second position	B minor	Eighth position	F minor
Third position	C minor	Ninth position	F♯ or G♭ minor
Fourth position	C♯ or D♭ minor	Tenth position	G minor
Fifth position	D minor	Eleventh position	G♯ or A♭ minor
Sixth position	D♯ or E♭ minor	Twelfth position	A minor

ASSIGNMENT

Play the melody to "Dark Eyes" and then play a jazz chorus using the runs learned so far.

Dark Eyes

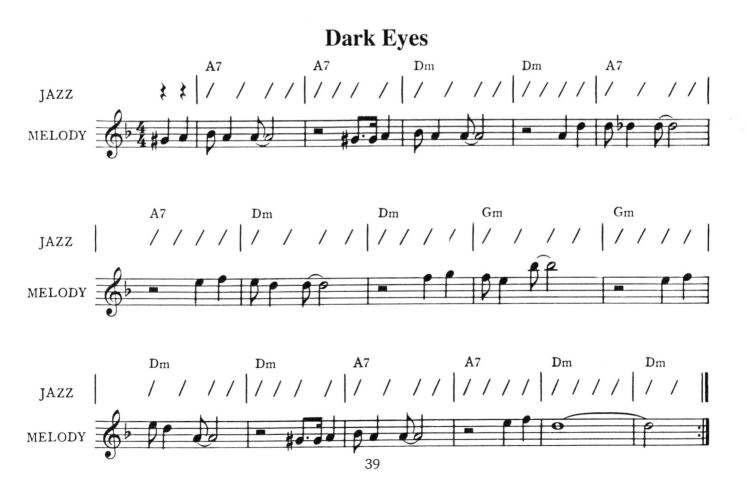

39

Even with the few runs learned, there are several ways the jazz chorus for "Dark Eyes" could be played. The following are examples.

JAZZ EXAMPLE 1

JAZZ EXAMPLE 2

JAZZ EXAMPLE 3

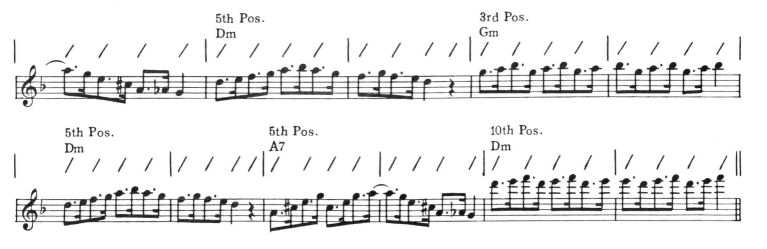

LESSON 9

We are now familiar with run forms for one major chord, two dominant seventh chords, and two minor chords.

By changing the time values of the notes in the runs learned thus far, we may multiply many times the five run forms already learned. What is more important, changing the time values will bring us another step closer to professional-sounding runs.

To illustrate how the note time values may be changed, we have shown below one of the original dominant seventh runs written as we presently play it. Following the original run are examples of how the note time values may be changed to give the run a completely new flavor.

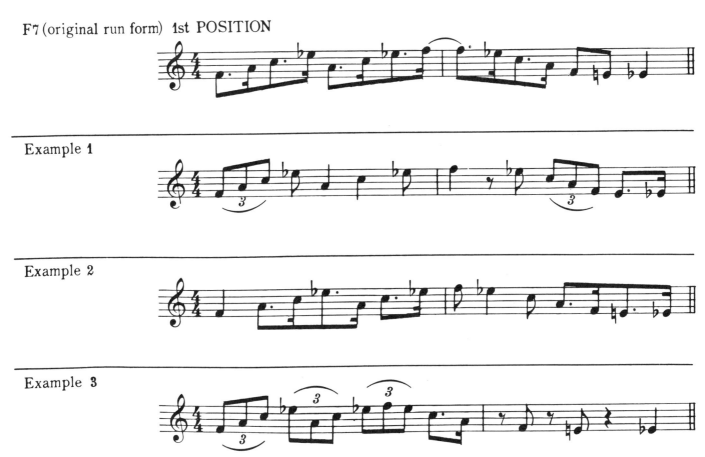

41

ASSIGNMENT

The student should purchase a music manuscript book for the purpose of starting a collection of runs.

Write the original major run in the manuscript book. Directly beneath the major run, write the same run but change the time values of the notes. It is permissible to add or delete notes of the run if you desire. After the run is written, it should be played on the guitar. The student should write several pages of major runs, each time changing the timing of the notes. If, in the process of playing one of the runs which you have written, you should "hear" something which may improve your creation, write your new idea on your sheet of run collections.

This process should be repeated many times for each run learned thus far (major, minor, and seventh runs). Upon completion of writing (and playing) several pages of runs, the student should memorize those runs that sound best to him or her and should learn them on all positions of the fingerboard. These selected runs should be fuller and better sounding than the basic runs which were presented previously. The new runs should be applied to many different songs in order to become familiar with them.

Not only is the student learning the basic aspects of playing jazz at this point but, as a result of writing his or her own runs, the student is also going through the process of developing a jazz style.

It must be stressed that the student should listen to as much jazz as possible while working through this book.

LESSON 10

As a result of changing the time values in the basic runs presented, the new runs should have somewhat more flavor. However, even if all the instruction presented thus far has been carried out to the letter, the student will find that his or her jazz solos are still quite stiff and unflowing. This stiffness may be overcome by the proper usage of passing tones.

A passing tone is a note not in the chord which may be played between one chord note and another chord note. Below are several examples of passing tones in a C major chord.

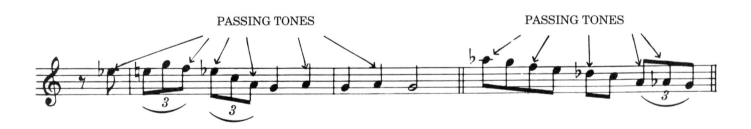

Upon looking over the examples set forth above, the student may have the feeling that "anything goes" and that there is no such thing as a wrong note. To a degree this is so, with one very important exception. *The chord sound must be established.*

The proper usage of passing tones may be likened to watching a movie on the screen. The film is comprised of many individual pictures. The individual pictures flash by so quickly that we are left with the impression of seeing one continuous picture depicting movement. When passing tones are properly used, the listener is not aware of the passing tones, but instead hears blending of the chord notes with the chord accompaniment.

The correct interweaving of passing tones with the chord tones and the use of an interesting rhythmic pattern (time values) will result in a smooth, pleasing jazz sound.

ASSIGNMENT

The student should write several pages of runs using passing tones. The best runs should then be memorized so that they can be played in all positions by sliding the left hand along the fingerboard while retaining the same fingering form.

Special care should be given to the application of this lesson, as the runs which the student composes and memorizes will be the framework for his or her individual jazz style.

The student should continue to listen to as much jazz as possible. The purpose of listening to jazz music is to enable the student to hear how jazz musicians "handle" the jazz solos for various tunes containing different chord progressions.

The student should copy solos which he or she hears by top-notch jazz musicians. As a result of copying solos, the student will achieve enough strength to go beyond the copying stage and finally arrive at the point where he or she will be able to freely play original jazz ideas. When this point is reached, the student should refrain from copying solos, for a truly good jazz musician creates his or her own solos.

LESSON 11

Quite frequently, the guitarist is called upon to play a jazz chorus on chords which change during the measure.

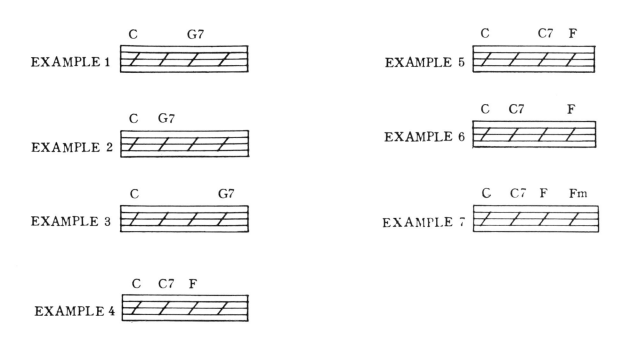

The student may improvise on chord changes within a measure in one of two ways. The first manner is that of using *common tones*. Common tones are those notes which are common to more than one chord. For example, the note G appears in the C major chord, and it also appears in the G7 chord.

If the note G were to be sounded while the accompaniment chords (C major and G7) were alternated

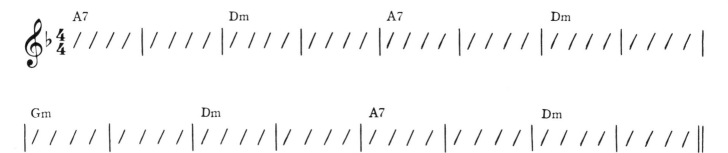

there would be perfect blending of the note G and the accompaniment chords. By determining the tone or tones common to the different chords which appear within the measure, the jazz musician has a basis upon which to play the jazz solo.

The jazz guitarist need not wait for a measure containing several chords to appear before making use of common tones. In the song "Dark Eyes" played earlier in this book, the chord progression is as follows.

The note A appears in both the A7 and D minor chords. Therefore, the common tone A may be sustained or repeated throughout the first eight measures. For the two measures of G minor, the musician may play a G minor run or one of the notes in the G minor chord (G B♭ D). The last six measures of "Dark Eyes" are composed of A7 and D minor. The common tone A may again be played for the last six measures of this song.

If this should appear:

the student may follow the same procedure outlined above.

Another example of how common tones may be used: The following is the chord progression for the first eight measures of a well-known standard song.

44

By using common tones it is possible to play the following jazz chorus based upon the previous chord progression. Notice that though the progression contains chord changes within the measures, only two notes (F and A) are used throughout the jazz chorus.

When using common tones as the basis for a jazz chorus or a portion of a jazz chorus, the student should also use a device known as *voice leading*.

Voice leading will be discussed in great detail in Part Two. For the present, however, voice leading will be defined as the playing of one note of the chord which will lead most smoothly to another note of the following chord.

Below is an example of voice leading using the jazz chorus written above.

Notice how each measure leads smoothly into the next measure of a properly voiced solo.

As mentioned earlier, there are two ways which a student may improvise on chord changes within a measure. The second manner in which jazz guitar solos may be played against measures containing more than one chord is by ignoring passing chords and basing the solo upon principal chords. A passing chord is one which is not absolutely necessary for the chord accompaniment. A passing chord will enrich the accompaniment by bridging the gap from one accompaniment chord to the next.

This procedure may be applied only when a passing chord receives one beat of the measure.

ASSIGNMENT

Write two jazz choruses based on the following progression. Play the two written jazz choruses. When this is done, the student should attempt to extemporaneously play jazz choruses based upon the progression.

Cmaj.7   C6   E7   E9   E7   Dm   Dm6   Dm   E7   D   Gm   E7

C   D7   D9   D13   D9   Dm7   G7   Cmaj.7   Em7   Ebm7   Dm7

C   C6   Cmaj.7   C6   Bm   Bm+   Bm7   Bm6   F   F6   Fm   Fm6

C6   D7   Dm7   Db7   C

C13   F7b5

D13   G7b5

C6   E7   Dm   Dm6   E7   E9   E7

Cmaj.7   Em7   Ebm7   Dm7   Dm9   G13   C

LESSON 12

The student should follow the same procedure outlined in Lesson 9. However, runs should be written for major 7, major 6, minor 7, minor 6, augmented and augmented 7, diminished 7, dominant 9, major 9, minor 9, dominant 13, and augmented 11.

The best runs for each chord should be memorized. Passing tones should be used freely. It is not necessary to include all of the chord notes in a run, provided that the chord sound is established. Runs may be as long or short as the student wishes. A run need not contain many notes to be effective. Many good jazz artists will often allow the rhythm section of the orchestra or group to aid the jazz solo by filling in the "breathing space" left open by the jazz soloist.

PART TWO
Chord Rhythm Playing & Substitutions

Author's Note

Ronny Lee

Of the many facets to guitar playing and of the various manners in which the guitar may be played (popular, classic, folk, flamenco, modern, progressive, etc.) the study of jazz chord accompaniment is one of the most fascinating.

The music theory studied in Part One will be put to good use in our study of chords. A knowledge of the entire fingerboard will prove to be extremely helpful but not an absolute necessity in the study of Part Two.

This section will show those chords which may appear on a guitar part, and also will go into great detail on the subject of chord substitution. The guitarist who thoroughly masters this section will be capable of meeting every requirement demanded of a top-notch rhythm accompanist.

Good luck and musical success,

Ronny Lee

LESSON 1

The Major Chord with the Root in the Bass

(Bass means the 6th string)

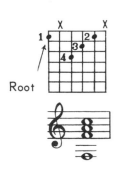

Root

POSITION	CHORD	BASS NOTE
1st position	F major	F
2nd position	F♯ or G♭ major	F♯ or G♭
3rd position	G major	G
4th position	G♯ or A♭ major	G♯ or A♭
5th position	A major	A
6th position	A♯ or B♭ major	A♯ or B♭
7th position	B major	B
8th position	C major	C
9th position	C♯ or D♭ major	C♯ or D♭
10th position	D major	D
11th position	D♯ or E♭ major	D♯ or E♭
12th position	E major	E

The student should practice the following exercise. To aid in learning the positions, the bass note for each chord is indicated.

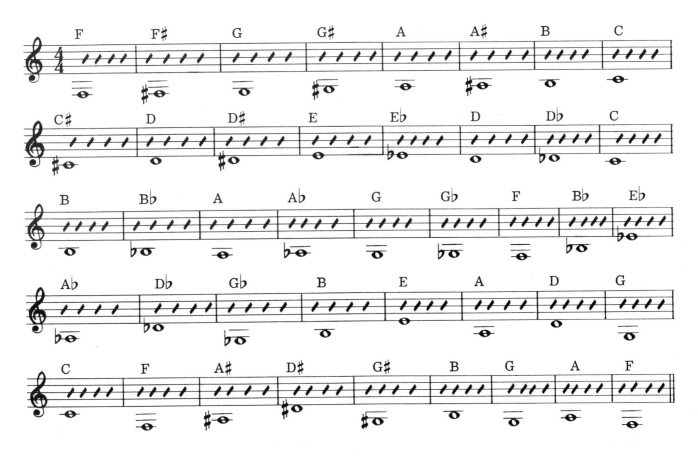

49

LESSON 2

The G major chord contains the notes G, B, and D. The G major 7 chord contains the notes G, B, D, and F♯. The G7 (dominant) contains the notes G, B, D, and F. The G6 chord contains the notes G, B, D, and E.

G major	G	B	D	
G major 7	G	B	D	F♯
G7	G	B	D	F
G6	G	B	D	E

By lowering the note played on the 4th string of the major chord, root in the bass, we can form the major 7, dominant 7, and major 6 chords.

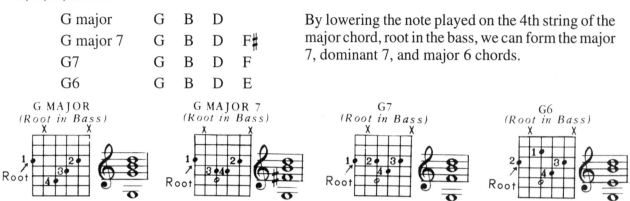

In all of the above chords, the notes on the 2nd, 3rd, and 6th strings are the same. The 1st and 5th strings are muted. Only the notes on the 4th string change to produce the major, major 7, dominant 7, or major 6 chords. The root of each of the four chords is in the bass (6th string).

The maj7, dom7, and maj6 chords may be moved up or down the fingerboard in the same manner applied to the root in the bass major in Lesson 1.

Exercise 1

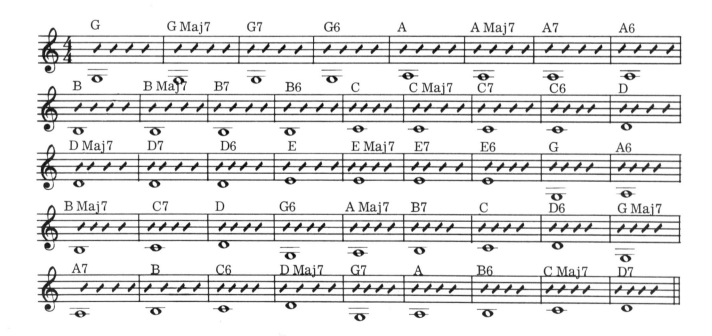

Exercise 2

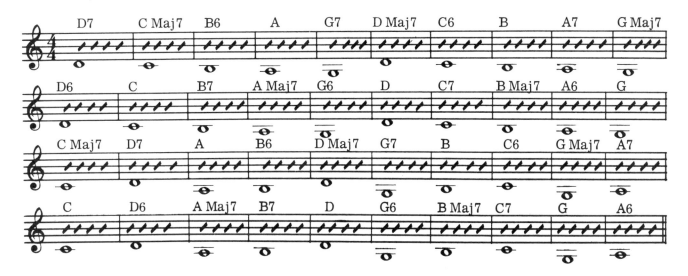

LESSON 3

The Major Chord with the Third in the Bass

POSITION	CHORD	BASS NOTE
1st position	D♯ or E♭ major	G
2nd position	E major	G♯ or A♭
3rd position	F major	A
4th position	F♯ or G♭ major	A♯ or B♭
5th position	G major	B
6th position	G♯ or A♭ major	C
7th position	A major	C♯ or D♭
8th position	A♯ or B♭ major	D
9th position	B major	D♯ or E♭
10th position	C major	E

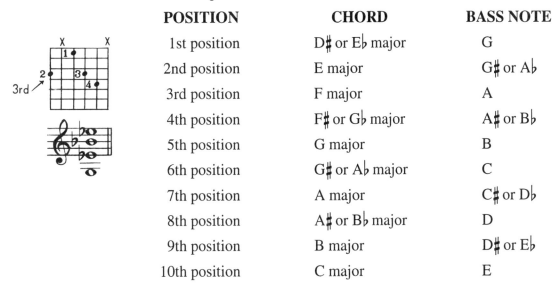

Exercise on the Major Chord (3rd in the Bass)

Observe the bass notes.

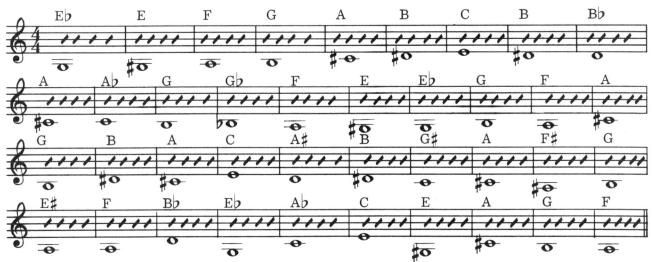

51

LESSON 4

The F major chord contains the notes F, A, and C. The F major 7 chord contains the notes F, A, C, and E. The F dominant 7 chord contains the notes F, A, C, and E♭. The F major 6 chord contains the notes F, A, C, and D.

F major	F	A	C	
F major 7	F	A	C	E
F7	F	A	C	E♭
F6	F	A	C	D

By lowering the note played on the 2nd string of the major chord, 3rd in the bass, we can form the major 7, dominant 7, and major 6 chords.

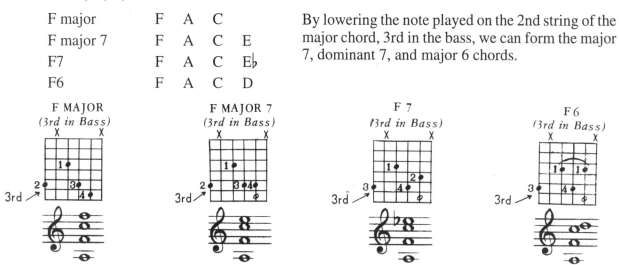

In all of the above chords, the notes on the 3rd, 4th, and 6th strings are the same. The 1st and 5th strings are muted. Only the notes on the 2nd string change to produce the major, major 7, dominant 7, or major 6 chords. The 3rd of each of the four chords is in the bass (6th string).

The maj7, dom7, and maj6 chords may be moved up or down the fingerboard in the same manner applied to the 3rd in the bass major in Lesson 3.

Exercise 1

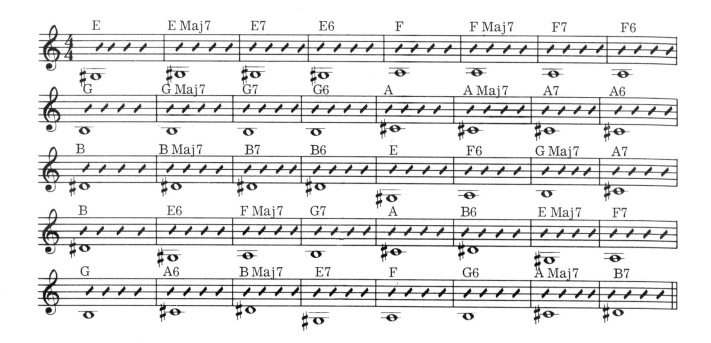

52

Exercise 2

Observe the bass notes.

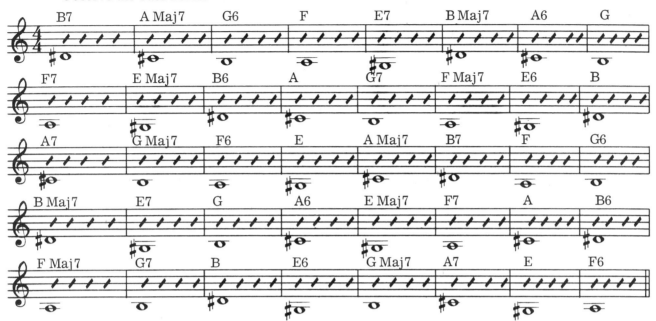

LESSON 5

The Major Chord with the Fifth in the Bass

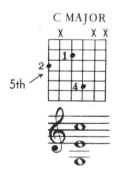

C MAJOR

POSITION	CHORD	BASS NOTE
1st position	B major	F♯ or G♭
2nd position	C major	G
3rd position	C♯ or D♭ major	G♯ or A♭
4th position	D major	A
5th position	D♯ or E♭ major	A♯ or B♭
6th position	E major	B
7th position	F major	C
8th position	F♯ or G♭ major	C♯ or D♭
9th position	G major	D
10th position	G♯ or A♭ major	D♯ or E♭
11th position	A major	E
12th position	A♯ or B♭ major	F

Exercise on the Major Chord (5th in the Bass)

Observe the bass notes.

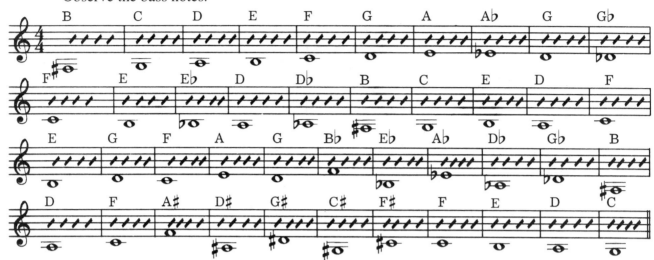

LESSON 6

The C major chord contains the notes C, E, and G. The C major 7 chord contains the notes C, E, G, and B. The C dominant 7 chord contains the notes C, E, G, and B♭. The C major 6 chord contains the notes C, E, G, and A.

C major	C	E	G	
C major 7	C	E	G	B
C7	C	E	G	B♭
C6	C	E	G	A

By lowering the note played on the 3rd string of the major chord, 5th in the bass, we can form the major 7, dominant 7, and major 6 chords. The student will observe that the root of the major 7 chord is omitted. This is an acceptable practice in chord voicing.

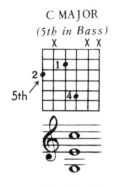
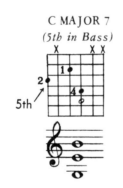
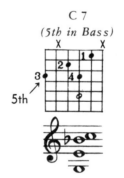
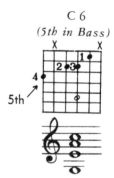

In all of the above chords the 5th is in the bass. Observe the muted strings. The major 7, dominant 7, and major 6 chords may be moved up or down the fingerboard in the same manner applied to the major chord with the 5th in the bass.

Exercise 1

54

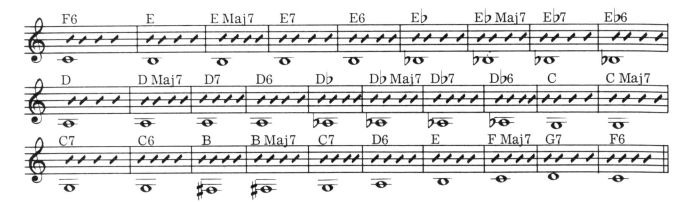

Exercise 2

Observe the bass notes.

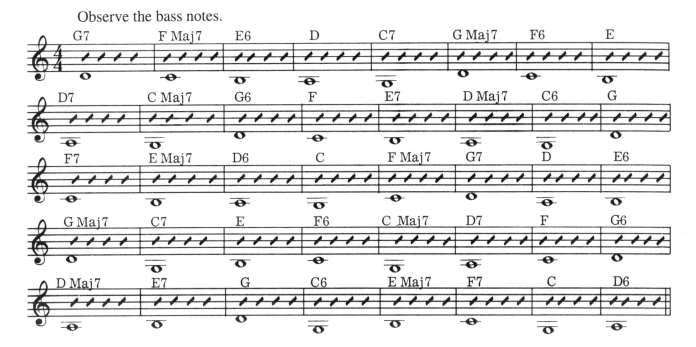

LESSON 7

The following exercise is to be played four times. The first time all chords should be played as majors, the second time as major 7ths, the third time as dominant 7ths, the fourth time as major 6ths.

Exercise on Chords Derived from the Major
(Root, 3rd, and 5th in the Bass)

LESSON 8
Exercise 1 (Root, 3rd, and 5th in the Bass Chords)

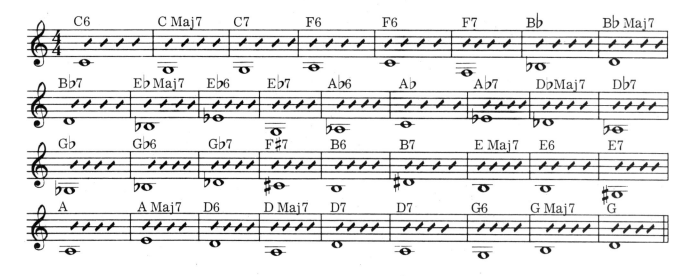

Exercise 2

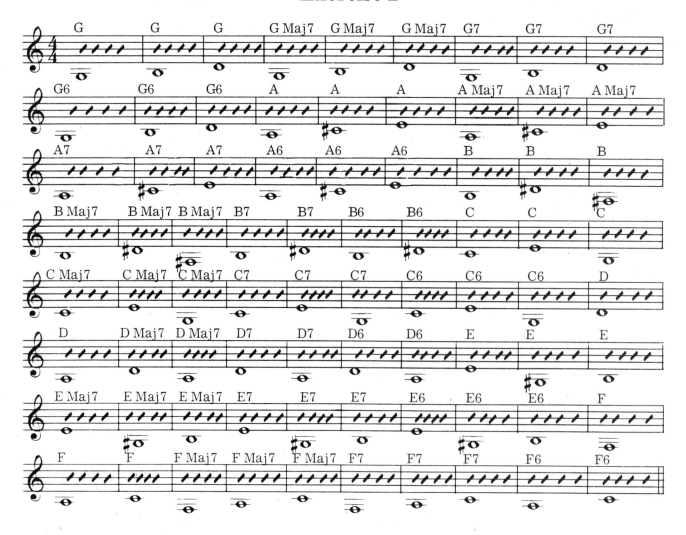

LESSON 9

CHORD SUBSTITUTION

It is the purpose of this course to teach the student the art of embellishing written chord accompaniment and to explain the manner in which monotonous repetition of the same chord over many measures may be avoided.

Obviously, if we wish to make an accompaniment more interesting, we must substitute different chords for those which appear in the music. However, the substitution of one chord for another is not the solution to an uninteresting accompaniment. For example, if a G major chord should appear in our music for 16 beats and in its place we use a G6 chord, the G6 chord will become as tiring as the original G major chord.

Fortunately, *more than one* chord may be used in place of a given chord. If a given chord appears for consecutive measures, we may choose as a substitution several of many chords to enrich the accompaniment. As a result, repetition is avoided and an interesting chord accompaniment is produced.

Every chord contains a letter name and a type name.

The letter name may be any letter in the musical alphabet (ABCDEFG). The letter name may be sharped or flatted.

The "type" names may be major, minor, or dominant. Examples of major-type chords are major 6, major 7, major 9, and major 6 add 9.

MAJOR CHORD SUBSTITUTION

When a major chord appears, we may use in its place any major-type chord of the same letter (root) name. This is called a *direct substitution.*

Two major-type chords studied thus far are the major 7 and major 6 chords.

Below is an exercise showing the given chords on the top lines and the substitution chords on the bottom lines. The student should thoroughly analyze the exercise and then practice the lines marked "Substitutions." It is important that the student observe all bass notes in order to play the correct inversion of each chord.

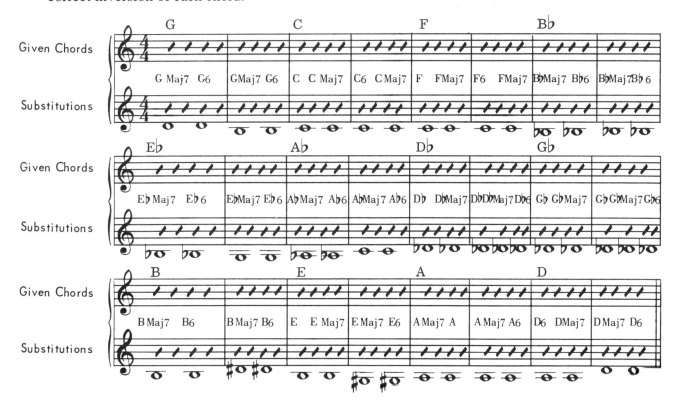

LESSON 10

The student should write substitution chords for the given chords. Bass notes are to be indicated. When the student has completed writing the substitution chords and bass notes, he or she should then practice playing the "Substitutions" lines which the student has written.

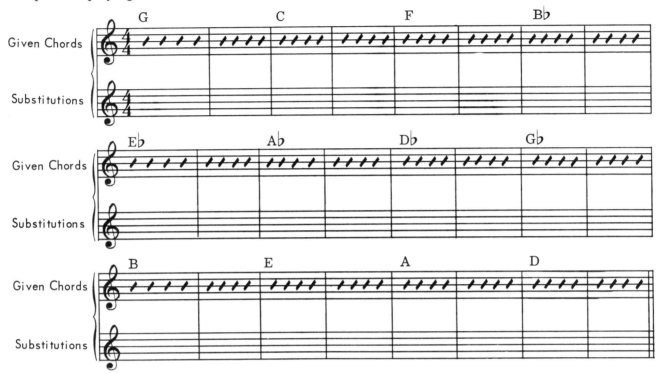

LESSON 11

DIRECT SUBSTITUTION FOR THE DOMINANT 7TH CHORD

When a dominant 7 chord appears, we may substitute any dominant 7-type chord which has the same root name as the given chord. Examples of dominant 7-type chords are: augmented 7, dominant 9, 13, dominant 7♯9, dominant 7♭9, dominant 7♭5, dominant 7 suspended, etc.

Because all of the dominant 7-type chords are derived from the dominant 7, it will be an easy matter for the student to assimilate all of the new chords.

Notice in the chord below that all movement occurs on the 2nd string while the other strings remain unchanged.

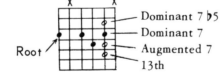

Fingerings Derived from the Dominant 7, Root in the Bass

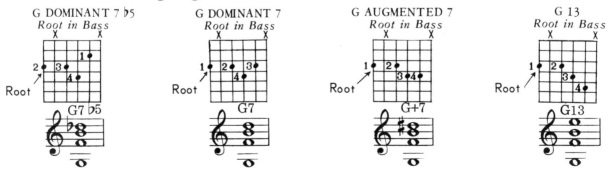

NOTE: The 13th chord is sometimes referred to as a dominant 7 add 6 or a dominant 9 add 6.

The upper lines of the following exercise show the given chords. The lower lines contain the substitution chords. The student should first analyze the usage of the substitutions and then practice playing the lower lines. All of the substitution chords in the exercise contain the root in the bass.

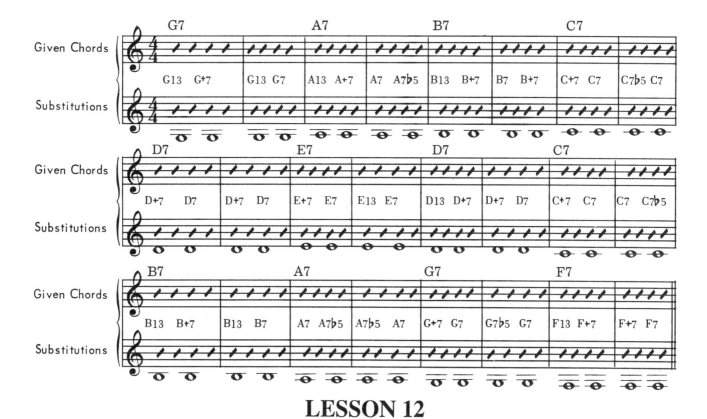

LESSON 12

THE DOMINANT 7TH SUSPENDED

The suspended chord is one in which the 3rd of the chord is raised one half step. When this occurs, the 3rd of the chord becomes the 4th. The notes in the G dominant 7th chord are G B D F.

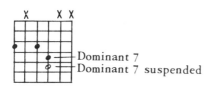

The notes in the dominant 7th suspended form are G C D F. The dominant suspended will usually resolve to a dominant 7 of the same root name. The major suspended will usually resolve to a major of the same root name. NOTE: To improve the facility of fingering the suspended chord, the 2nd string is omitted. To attain the best voicing when resolving the suspended to the dominant, the 2nd string is omitted on the dominant 7th.

Dominant 7 Suspended Derived from the Dominant 7, Root in the Bass

The upper lines of the exercise below show the given chords. The lower lines contain the substitution chords. The student should first analyze the usage of the substitutions and then practice playing the lower lines. All of the substitution chords below contain the root in the bass.

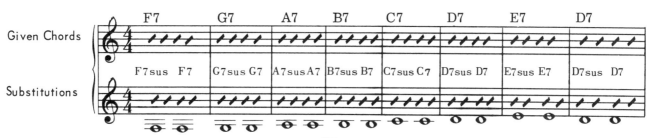

59

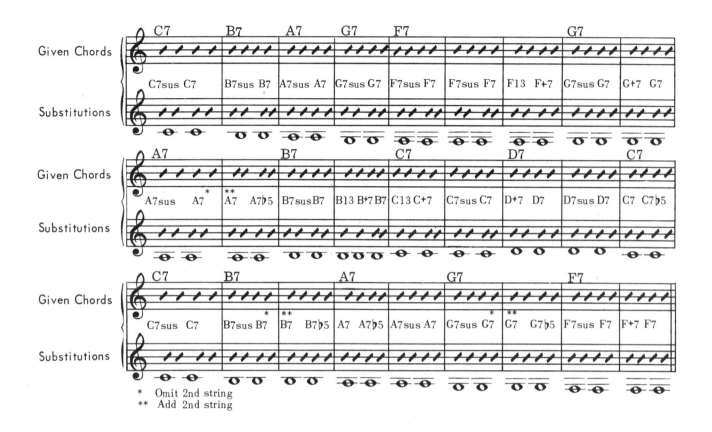

* Omit 2nd string
** Add 2nd string

LESSON 13

SUBSTITUTION CHORDS DERIVED FROM THE DOMINANT 7TH CHORD WITH THE FIFTH IN THE BASS

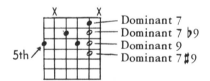

Dominant 7
Dominant 7 ♭9
Dominant 9
Dominant 7 ♯9

Notice that all movement occurs on the 2nd string while the other strings remain unchanged.

Fingerings Derived from the Dominant 7th, Fifth in the Bass

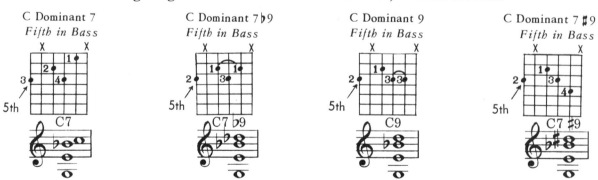

The upper lines of the following exercise show the given chords. The lower lines contain the substitution chords. The student should first analyze the usage of the substitutions and then practice playing the lower lines. All of the substitution chords below contain the 5th in the bass.

LESSON 14

The Suspended Chord Derived from the Dominant 7th with the Fifth in the Bass

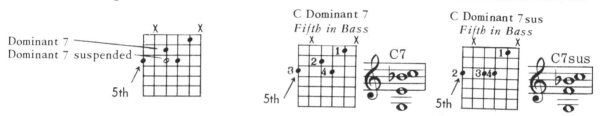

The Dominant 7th♭5 Derived from the Dominant 7th with the Fifth in the Bass

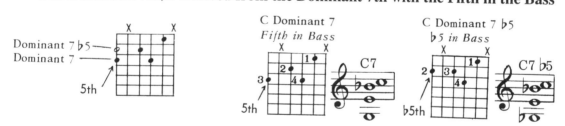

Exercise on Dominant 7th, Suspended 7th, and 7♭5 Chords

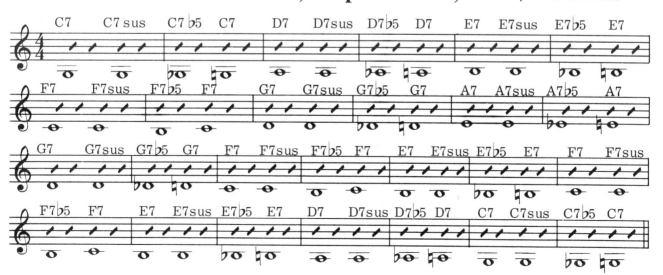

LESSON 15

THE DOMINANT 7♭5 CHORD

The 7♭5 chord may be played in two positions. For example, C7♭5 may be played in the first position and also (with the same fingering) in the 7th position.

The 7♭5 may have the root in the bass (♭5 on the 2nd string) or the ♭5 in the bass (root on the 2nd string).

Each 7♭5 fingering has two names. For example, D7♭5 is the same as A♭7♭5; F7♭5 is the same as B7♭5.

In the illustration below are all the 7♭5 chords and their alternate names. Notice that each 7♭5 chord is a flatted fifth higher (or lower) than its alternate name. For example, D7♭5 is a flatted fifth higher (or lower) than A♭7♭5; A♭7♭5 is a flatted fifth higher (or lower) than D7♭5.

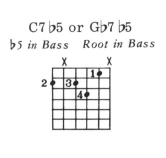

C7♭5 or G♭7♭5
♭5 in Bass   Root in Bass

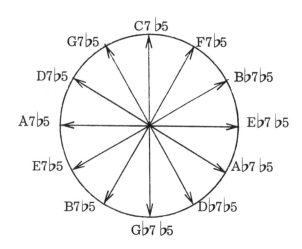

Exercise on the Dominant 7♭5, Root in the Bass and ♭5 in the Bass

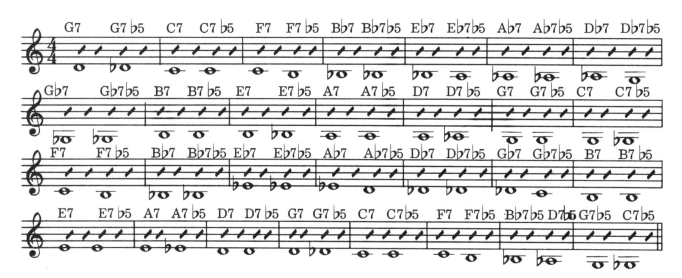

LESSON 16

DOMINANT 7TH SUBSTITUTION

When a dominant 7th chord appears we may count up a flatted 5th from the given chord and play a dominant 7th-type chord.

Examples of Dominant 7th Substitution Using the ♭5th Higher Technique

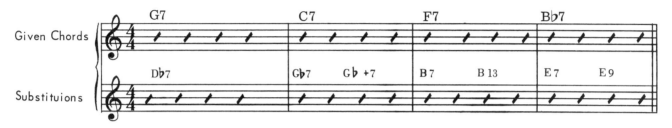

Below is a chord progression which may be seen in many songs. The student should analyze the usage of the substitutions and then practice playing the substitution lines.

The student should understand the "reason" for each substitution chord. It is extremely important that all bass notes be observed.

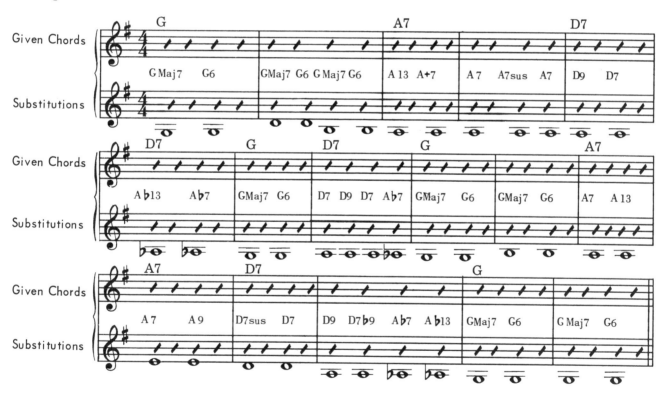

LESSON 17

Understand the "reason" for each substitution chord below and then practice playing the substitution lines in this very often-used chord progression.

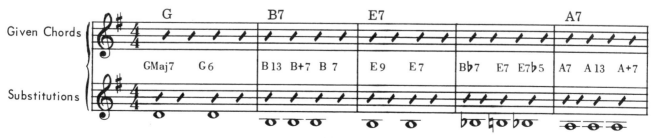

63

LESSON 18

APPLYING SUBSTITUTIONS TO THE I-VI-II-V PROGRESSIONS IN VARIOUS KEYS

Understand and practice all substitution lines below. Observe all bass notes.

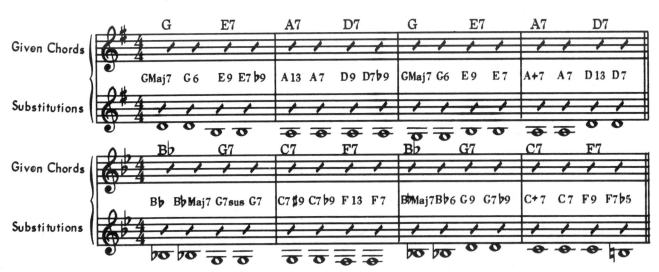

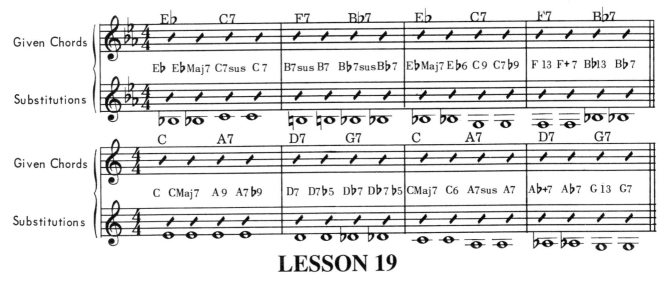

LESSON 19

ANOTHER MAJOR FORM AND DERIVATIONS, WITH THE ROOT IN THE BASS

Though the student is already familiar with the major chord, root in the bass, still another form is presented in order to add more color to our chord substitutions. Because this new major form necessitates a larger left-hand "stretch" than the previously learned form, we shall differentiate between the two root-in-the-bass major forms by referring to the new chord as the "big-stretch" major with the root in the bass.

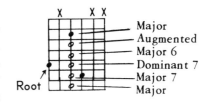

Fingering Derived from the Big-Stretch Major Chord, with the Root in the Bass

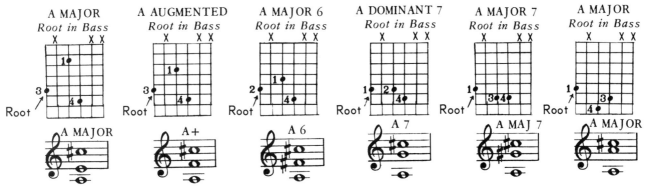

NOTE: The augmented chord is a major-type chord and may be used as a direct substitution for the major chord. However, the augmented 7th chord learned previously is a dominant-type chord and may be used as a direct substitution for a dominant 7th chord.

Exercise on Chords Derived from the Big-Stretch Major Chord

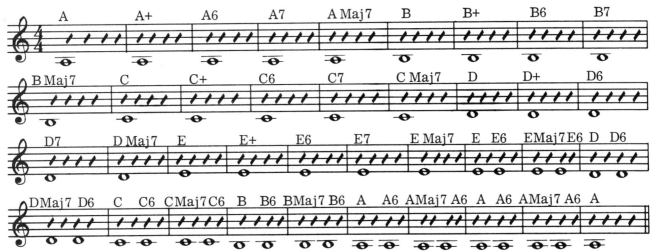

65

LESSON 20

THE AUGMENTED CHORD

The C augmented chord contains the notes C E G♯ (A♭).

The E augmented chord contains the notes E G♯ (A♭) C.

The G♯ (A♭) augmented chord contains the notes G♯ (A♭) C E.

The student will observe that the same three notes are contained in the C augmented, E augmented, and G♯ (A♭) augmented.

Any note in the augmented chord may be considered the root of the chord. Therefore, each augmented fingering will have three possible names.

When observing the chord diagrams below, notice that the augmented chord is derived by raising the 5th of the major chord one half step.

If an augmented chord precedes or follows a major chord with the 3rd in the bass, and if both the major chord and the augmented chord possess the same root name, then we will not finger the 2nd string of the major chord. We do this in order to attain the best possible chord voicing.

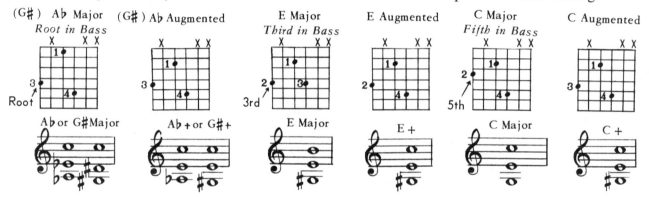

Augmented Exercise

All root-in-the-bass majors below are the "big-stretch" form. On all 3rd-in-the-bass majors below, the second string is unfingered and muted.

66

LESSON 21

MINOR PROGRESSIONS   ROOT IN THE BASS

Notice in the minor chord below that the note played on the fourth string is raised by half steps to form the minor augmented, minor 6, minor 7, and minor major 7 chord.

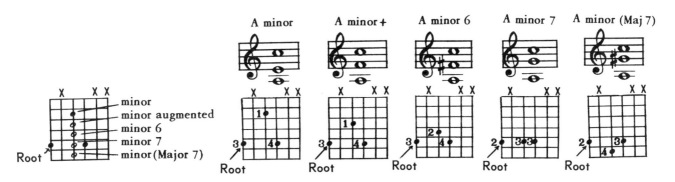

In order to obtain the best possible voicing, it is advantageous at times to use the optional fingerings for the root-in-the-bass minor 6 and minor 7 chords.

Optional Fingerings for Minor 6 and Minor 7 Chords

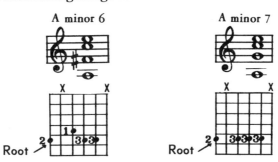

Minor Chord Exercise   Root in the Bass

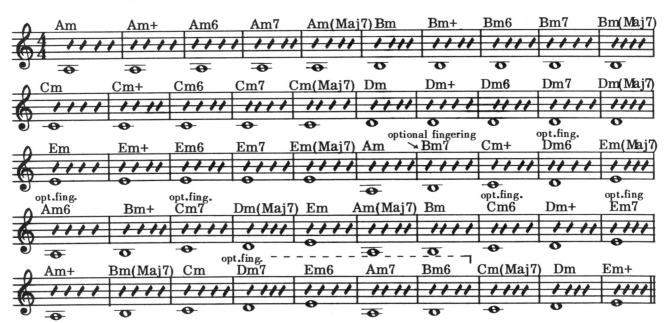

LESSON 22

MINOR PROGRESSIONS   THIRD IN THE BASS

Notice in the minor chord below that the note played on the second string is lowered by half steps to form the minor (maj7), minor 7, and minor 6 chord.

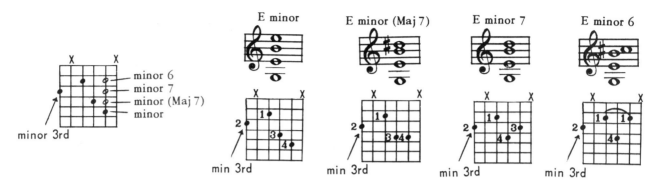

In order to obtain the best possible voicing, it is advantageous at times to use the optional fingering for the third in the bass minor form.

Optional Fingering for the Third in the Bass Minor Chord

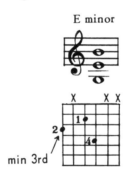

Minor Chord Exercise   Third in the Bass

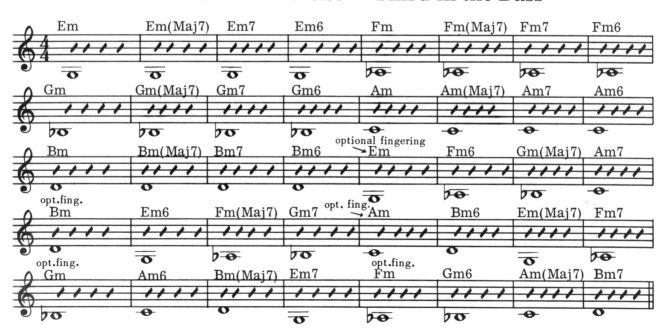

68

Another Minor Chord Exercise   Third in the Bass

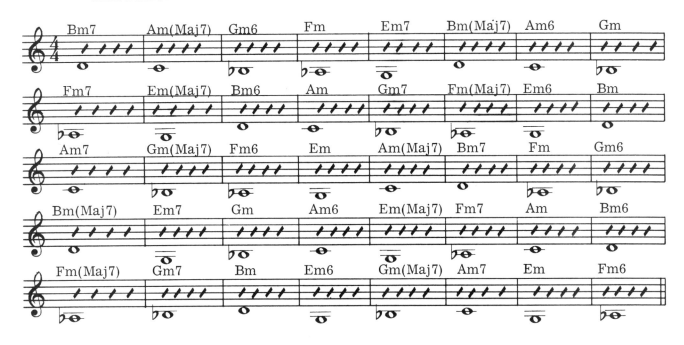

LESSON 23

Exercise on the Minor 7 and Minor 6 Chords   Third in the Bass

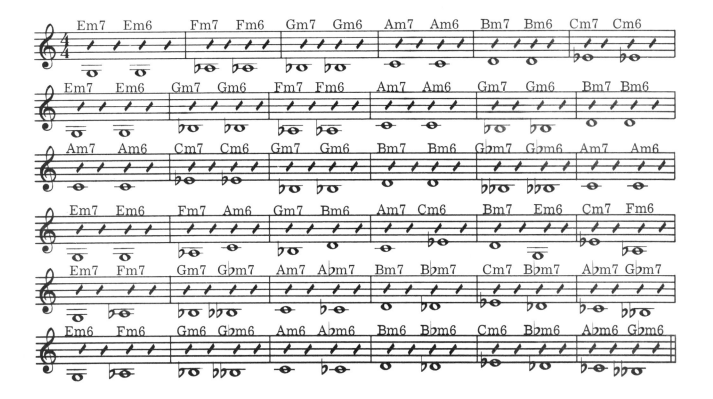

LESSON 24

MINOR PROGRESSIONS   FIFTH IN THE BASS

Notice in the minor chord below that the note played on the third string is lowered by half steps to form the minor (maj7), minor 7, and minor 6 chord.

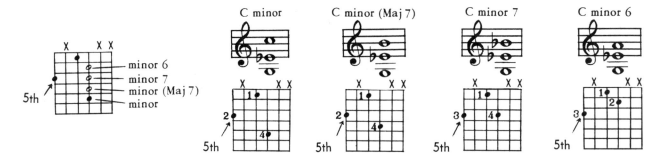

In order to obtain the best possible voicing, it is advantageous at times to use the optional fingerings for the fifth in the bass forms of the minor 7 and minor 6 chords.

Optional Fingerings for the Fifth-in-the-Bass Minor 7 and Minor 6 Chords

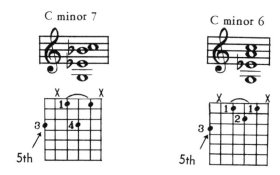

Exercise on the Minor Chords with the Fifth in the Bass

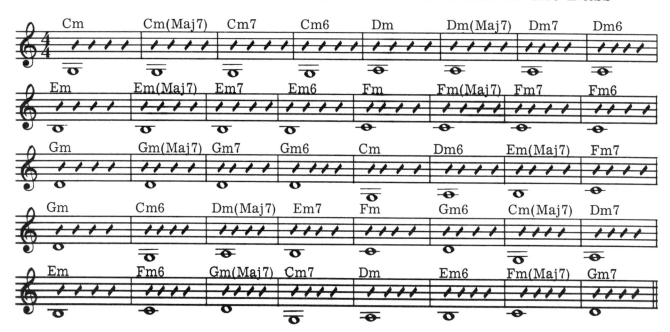

Another Exercise on the Minor Chords with the Fifth in the Bass

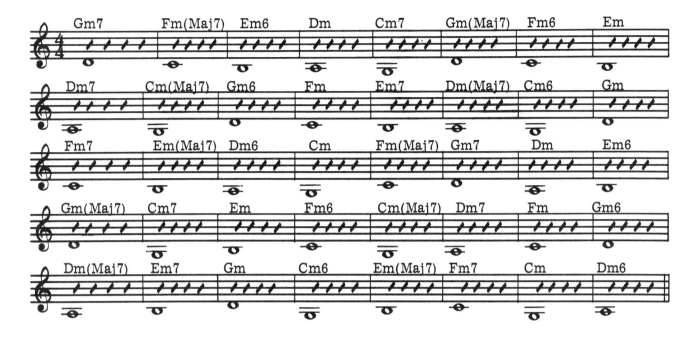

LESSON 25

Exercise on Minor 6 Chords with the Minor Third and Fifth in the Bass

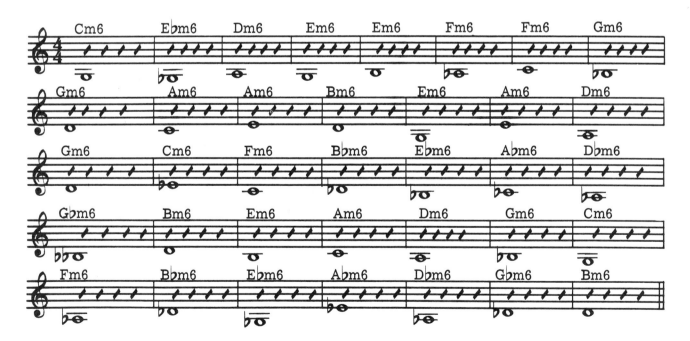

LESSON 26
SUBSTITUTIONS

When a minor chord appears in our music we may, by virtue of direct substitution, play a minor augmented, minor 6, minor (maj7), minor 7, or any minor-type chord of the same root name as the given chord.

We may also make good use of minor-type chords to aid us with additional substitutions for the major and dominant 7 chords.

When a dominant 7 chord appears, we may count up an interval of a fifth and substitute a minor-type chord.

EXAMPLE:

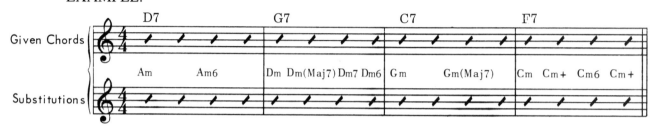

Important fingering information: The chord fingerings presented are subject to change. For example, if a minor (maj7) chord is followed by a minor 6 chord, both with the root in the bass:

and the guitarist wishes to use the three-note forms (as opposed to the optional fingerings), then this fingering:

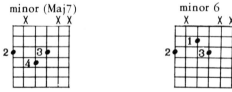

is much more practical than this fingering:

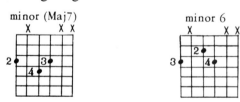

Because some chord fingerings are more comfortable when used in one progression than another, the student should exercise judgment in varying the fingerings set forth.

ANOTHER EXAMPLE:

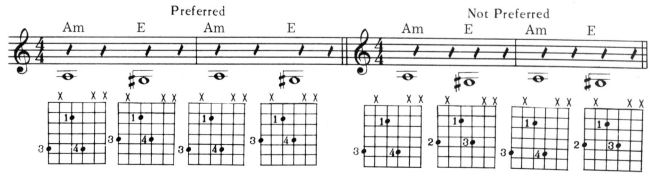

Important voicing information: When a chord progression contains a three-note chord, all other chords in that progression should also be three-note chords, unless the guitarist feels it advantageous to use a four-note chord.

The guitarist should exercise judgment in applying the best possible voicing for each progression.

EXAMPLE:

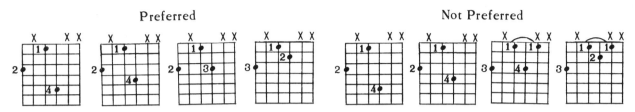

EXAMPLE:

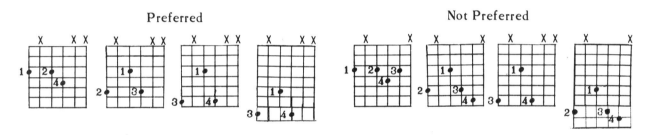

EXAMPLE:

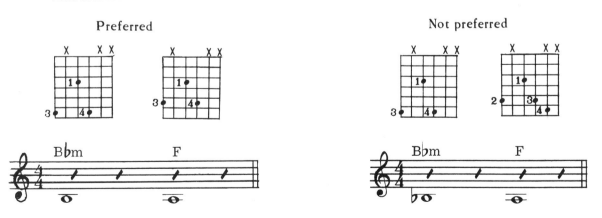

The following are two progressions showing the original chords and the substitution chords. The student should analyze the progressions and understand the "reason" for each substitution. The substitution lines should then be practiced until the student can play them smoothly.

Progression 1

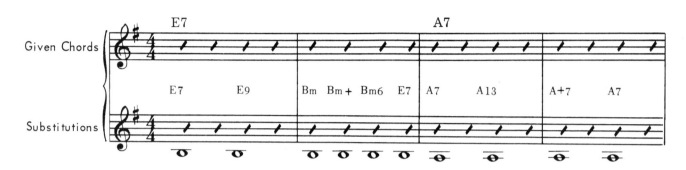

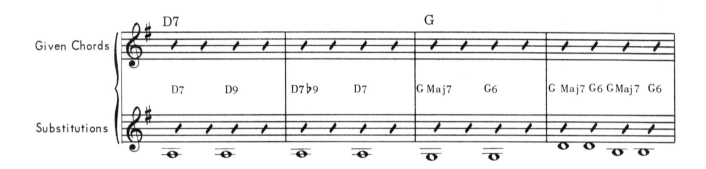

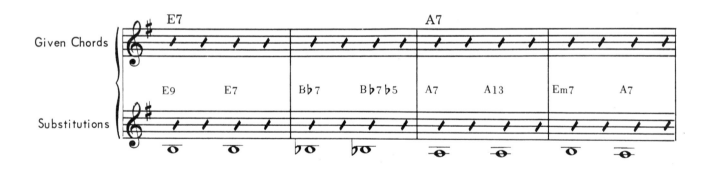

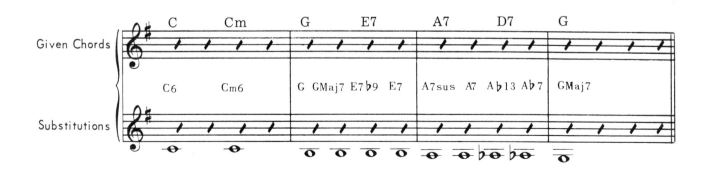

Progression 2

LESSON 27

Major Substitutions Review

When a major chord appears, we may substitute any major-type chord of the same root name as the given chord. This is called a direct substitution, and consists of alteration of the given chord.

Dominant 7 Substitutions Review

1. When a dominant 7 chord appears, we may substitute any dominant-type chord bearing the same root name as the give chord. This is called a direct substitution, and consists of alteration of the given chord.

2. When a dominant 7 chord appears we may substitute a dominant-type chord which is a flatted 5th higher than the given chord.

3. When a dominant 7 chord appears we may substitute a minor-type chord which is a 5th higher than the given chord.

Minor Substitutions Review

When a minor chord appears, we may substitute a minor-type chord bearing the same root name as the given chord. This is called a direct substitution, and consists of the given chord.

Another Major Substitution

When a major chord appears, we may play a scalewise progression of chords up to the 3rd degree of the scale. The 1st degree is major; the 2nd and 3rd degrees are minor.

Example of Scalewise Progression Up to the Third Degree

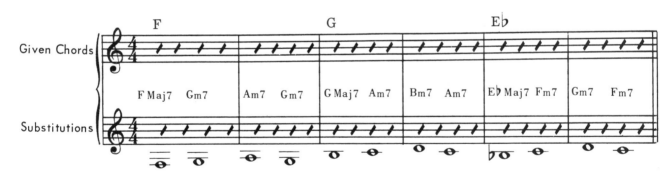

It is also acceptable to use the scalewise progression out of ascending scalewise order.

EXAMPLE:

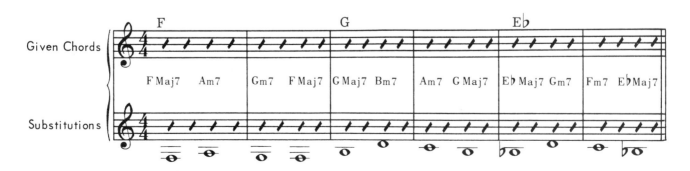

76

If desirable, the scalewise progression may be played only as high as the 2nd degree of the scale.

EXAMPLE:

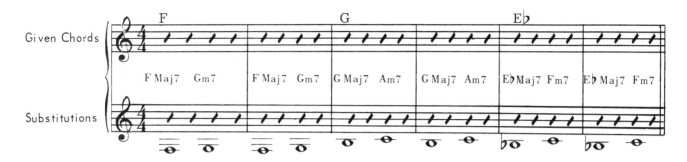

Although infrequent, the scalewise progression may be played up to the 4th degree of the scale. The 4th degree may be either major or minor, depending upon which will better blend with the melody line.

EXAMPLE:

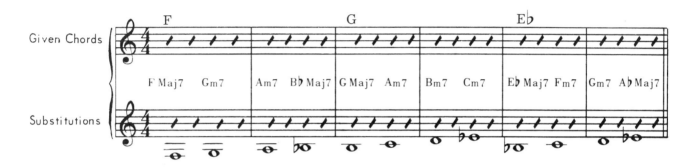

When using the scalewise major substitution progression in descending from the 3rd degree, we may progress by half steps.

EXAMPLE:

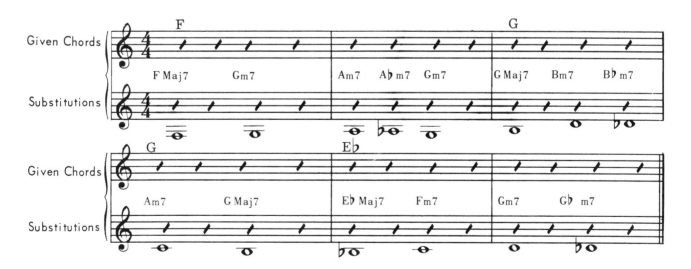

When a chord is followed by another chord of the same type which is one tone lower than the first chord, we may descend by half steps.

We may also apply the above rule when a major chord is followed by a dominant 7, which is a fifth higher than the major.

EXAMPLE:

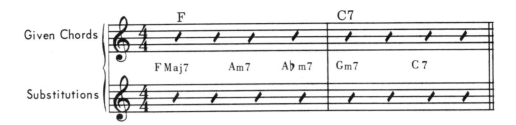

In the example above, we substituted F major 7 for the F major by virtue of direct substitution. We substituted A minor 7 for F major by virtue of the scalewise progression, out of scalewise order. We substituted A♭ minor 7 for F major because of the rule above; Am7 and Gm7 are one tone apart and are the same type of chord, and therefore we may descend by half steps. We substituted Gm7 for C7 because we may count up a 5th and substitute a minor chord in place of a dominant 7-type chord.

When a major chord appears, we may count up a third and play a minor-type chord.

EXAMPLE:

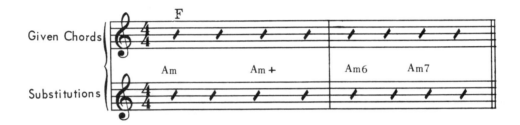

Play all substitution lines and understand the reason for each substitution.

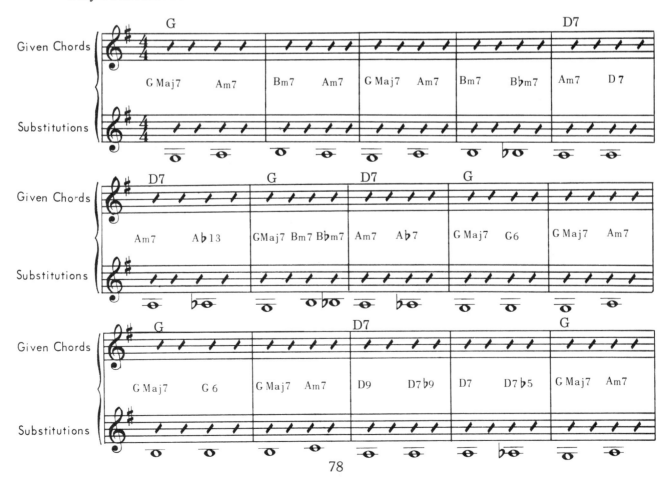

78

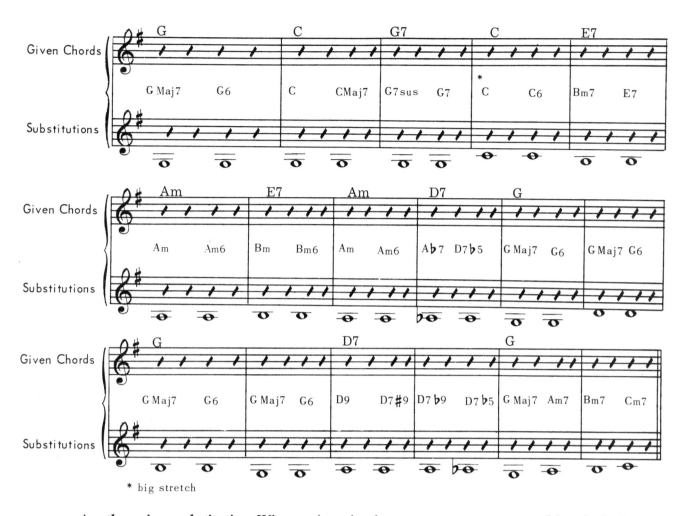

*big stretch

Another minor substitution: When a minor chord appears, we may count up a 5th and substitute a dominant-type chord. This substitution should be used very carefully in order to avoid any clash with the melody.

79

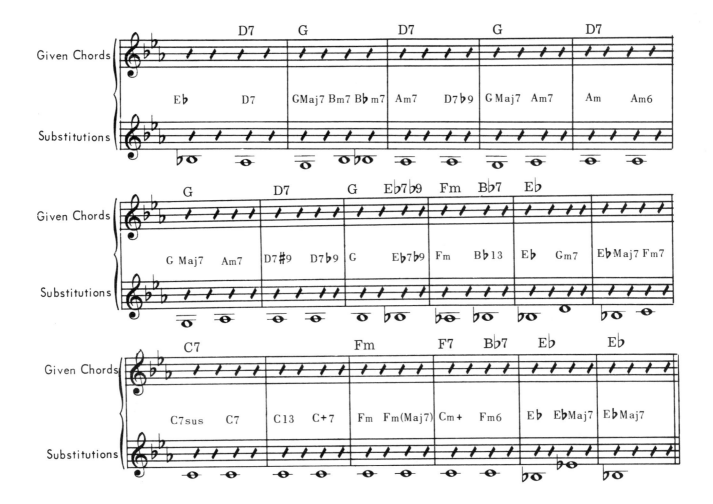

LESSON 28

Minor Form with the Root, Major 7, Minor 7, and Major 6 in the Bass

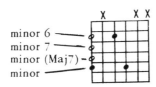

Fingerings

LESSON 29

THE DIMINISHED CHORD (DIM—°)

In popular music the diminished chord and the diminished 7 chord are the same.

The C diminished chord contains the notes C Eb Gb A.

The Eb diminished chord contains the notes Eb Gb A C.

The Gb diminished chord contains the notes Gb A C Eb.

The A diminished chord contains the notes A C Eb Gb.

The student will observe that the same four notes are contained in the C diminished, Eb diminished, Gb diminished, and A diminished.

Each diminished fingering will have four possible names. Any note in the diminished chord can be the root.

The student will bear in mind that the diminished chord is derived by lowering by one half step the 3rd, 5th, and 7th of the dominant 7 chord.

Deriving the Diminished Chord from the Dominant 7 Chord

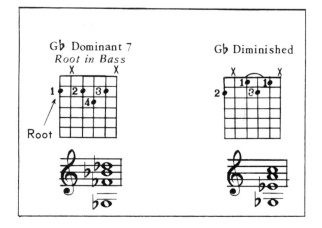

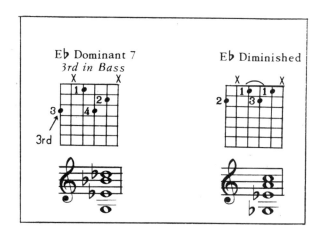

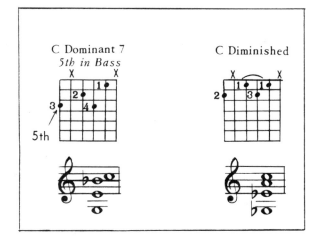

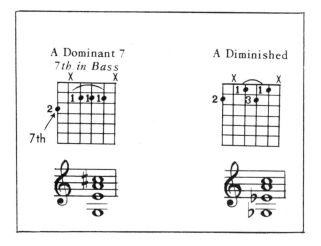

Diminished Exercise No. 1

Diminished Exercise No. 2

LESSON 30

VOICING SUGGESTION

When a major chord is followed by a diminished chord, and the diminished chord bears the same *root name* as the major chord, it is advisable, if practical, to use the major form with the 3rd in the bass. It is also suggested that only the three-string forms of both the major and diminished chords be used when appearing in this sequence (Example 1).

If, however, the major chord and diminished chord are not of the same root name, it is advisable to use the four-string forms for both chords. If the major chord is a major-type chord (other than major) bearing the same root name as the diminished, the four-string forms should be used (Example 2) if possible.

EXAMPLE 1:

Major chord followed by a diminished chord of the same root name.

EXAMPLE 2:

Major-type chord (other than major) followed by a diminished chord of the same root name.

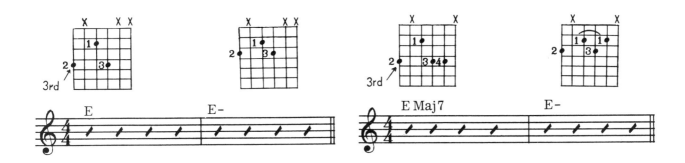

When a major-type chord is followed by a diminished chord which is one half step higher than the major, it is advisable, if practical, to use the major form with the root in the bass.

EXAMPLE:

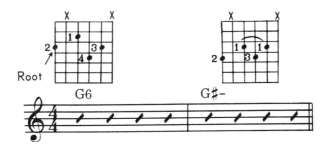

Substitution Suggestions

When a major chord is followed by a diminished chord, and the diminished chord bears the same *root name* as the major chord, it is acceptable to substitute for the major chord a minor 7 chord which is a 3rd higher than the major. For the diminished chord, we may substitute a minor 7 chord which is one half step lower than the minor 7 chord which was substituted for the major chord.

EXAMPLE:

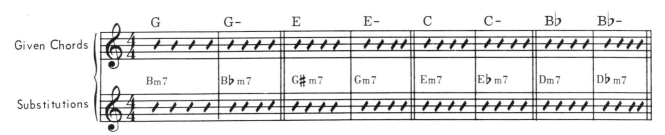

Exercise Based Upon a Chord Progression

Exercise Based Upon a Chord Progression

Notice how full and rich the substitution lines sound as a result of proper chord voicing and substitution.

LESSON 31

Dominant 13 Chord and Augmented 9 Chord (Derived from Dominant 9, Fifth in Bass)

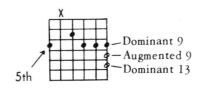

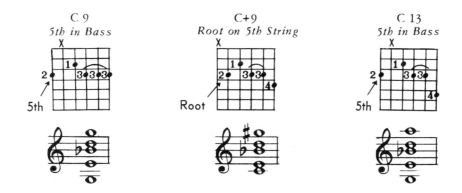

Exercise on Dominant 9, 13, and Augmented 9

(Note: Aug 9 bass note is on 5th string.)

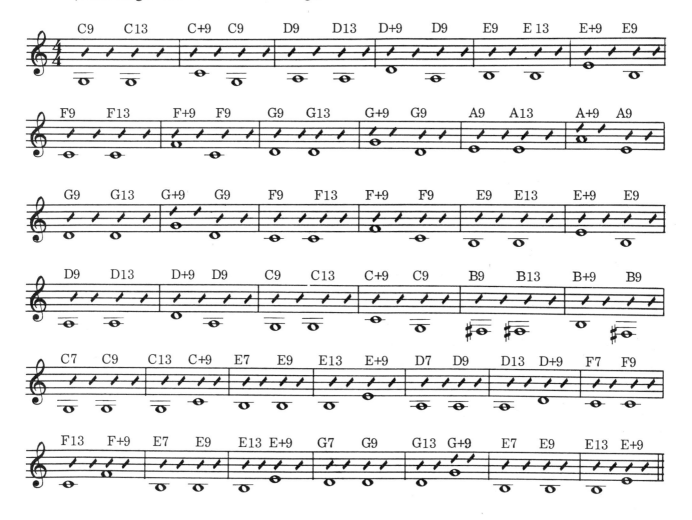

Augmented 9, Augmented 7♯9, Augmented 7♭9
(Derived from Augmented 7, Root in the Bass)

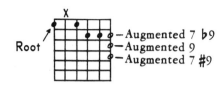

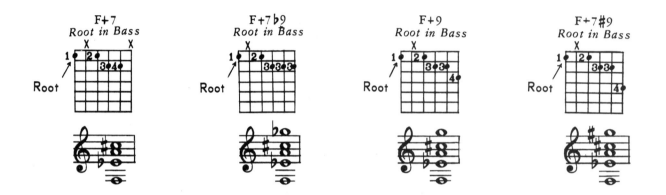

Exercise on Augmented 7, Augmented 7♭9, Augmented 7♯9, and Augmented 9 (Root in the Bass)

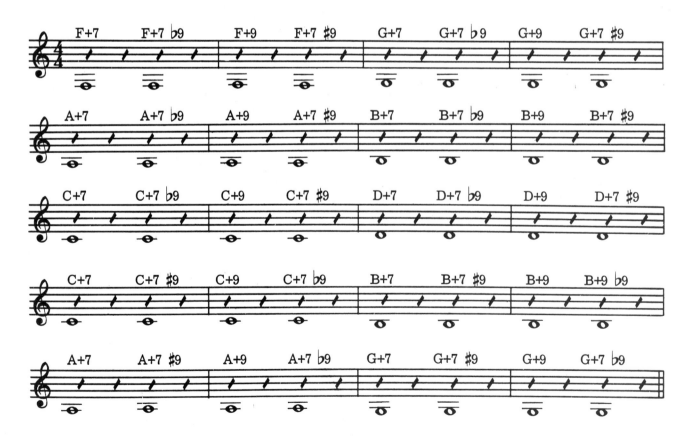

LESSON 32

The Major 9 Chord (with the Fifth in the Bass)

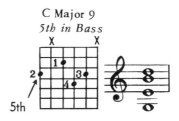

The major 9 is a major-type chord and may be used as a substitution for a major, major 7, major 6, or any major-type chord.

Exercise on the Major 9 Chord

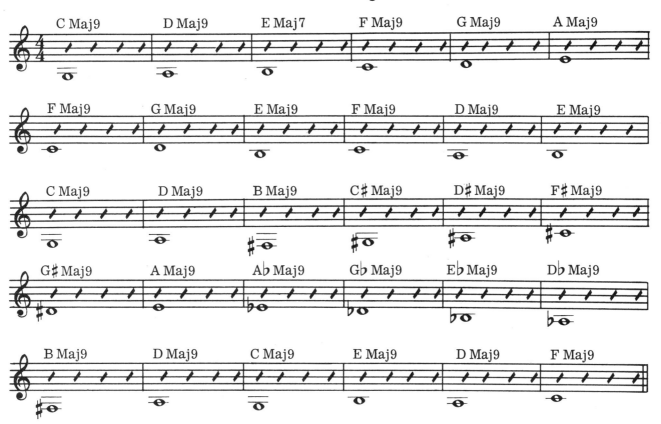

Two Minor 9 Forms

Substitution information: An augmented 7 chord is a substitution chord for a dominant 7. An augmented 9, augmented 7♭9, and augmented 7♯9 are substitution chords for an augmented 7. It is therefore acceptable to substitute any of the augmented 7 alterations for a dominant 7 by virtue of direct substitution.

The minor 9 chord is a substitution for the minor 7. As a result the minor 9 chord may be used as a substitution chord wherever it is practical to use a minor 7 chord as a substitution. For example, if C7 appears, we may substitute a G minor 7. Therefore, if C7 appears we may substitute a G minor 9. Actually, we are using a substitution chord for a substitution chord.

Exercise Employing the Minor 9 (with the Root in the Bass)

Understand all substitutions.

90

Exercise Employing the Minor 9 (Fifth in the Bass)

Understand all substitutions.

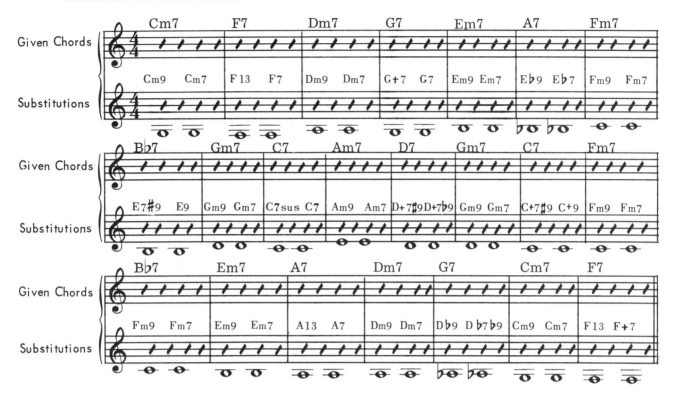

LESSON 33

Play the substitution lines in the progression below and understand the substitutions.

91

LESSON 34

The Minor 7♭5 Chord Derived from the Minor 7 Chord

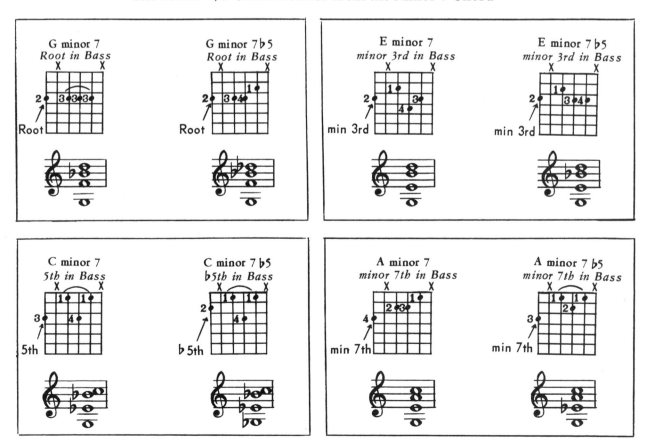

92

The student may quickly locate the minor 7♭5 chord by fingering the minor 7 chord and then lowering the 5th by one fret.

The minor 7♭5 chord is a substitution for a minor 7 chord.

The Dominant 7♯9

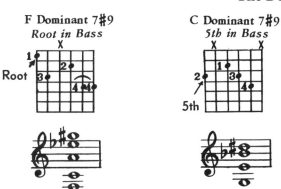

For purposes of substitution, the dominant 7♯9 may be treated in the same manner as any dominant-type chord.

The Major 6 Add 9

For purposes of substitution, the major 6 add 9 may be treated in the same manner as any major-type chord.

To avoid confusion, it is necessary to point out that a 6 add 9 chord is a major-type chord derived from the major 6. However, the 9 add 6 chord is a dominant-type chord derived from the 9th. The dominant 9 add 6 is another name for a 13th chord.

Exercise on the Dominant 7♯9 Chord and the Major 6 Add 9 Chord (Root in the Bass)

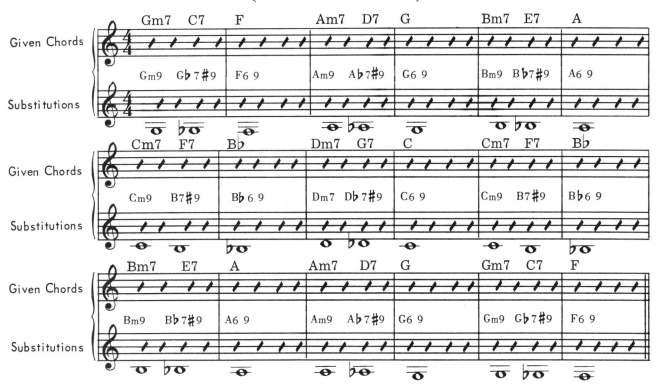

93

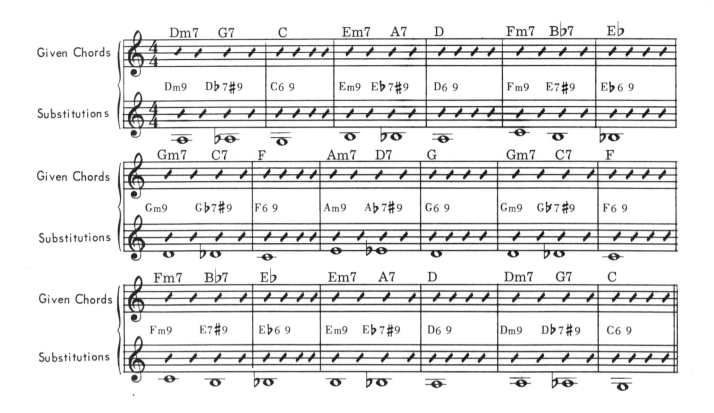

LESSON 35

Note: For purposes of substitution the 13♭9 chord is to be treated as a dominant-type chord.

Note: The 13♭9 chord, with the ♭9 in the bass, is fingered the same as the dominant 7♯9 with the 5th in the bass.

Exercise on the 13♭9 Chord

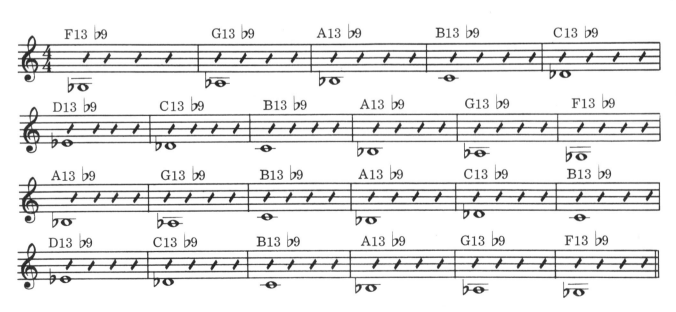

Minor 9 (Fifth in Bass) to 13♭9 (♭9 in Bass)

HINT: Move only the 2nd and 3rd fingers when progressing from min9 to 13♭9.

The Augmented 11 Chord (Also Referred to as the 9♭5 Chord)

The augmented 11 chord is the only augmented-type chord in which the augmented note *is not* the 5th of the chord. As may be seen above, the augmented note is the 11th of the chord.

The augmented 11 chord is the same as the dominant 9♭5 chord.

Substitution information: The dominant 9♭5 may at times be used as a substitution chord for a dominant 9 chord (direct substitution).

95

Three Ways to Use the Augmented 11 in Chord Substitution

1. As a direct substitution for a major chord. This should be done sparingly. This manner of substitution is used to its best advantage when the augmented 11 is played as the last chord of a song ending.

2. For a dominant 7, count up a flatted fifth and play augmented 11.

3. For a minor chord which is built upon the 4th degree of the scale of the key in which the music is being played, count up a 4th and play the augmented 11. It is also acceptable to use a 13th or 7♭5 chord for the minor built upon the 4th degree of the scale.

For example, in the key of C, if an F minor appears (4th scale degree), we may substitute a B flat augmented 11 (or B♭13 or B♭7♭5). In the key of G, if a C minor appears (4th scale degree), we may count up a 4th and substitute F augmented 11 (or F13 or F7♭5).

EXAMPLE:

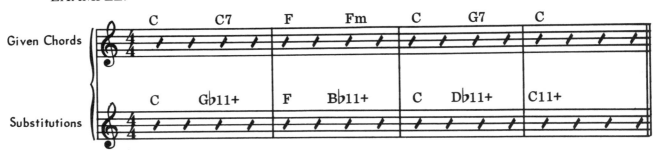

Exercise Based Upon a Well-Known Chord Progression

Understand all substitutions.

96

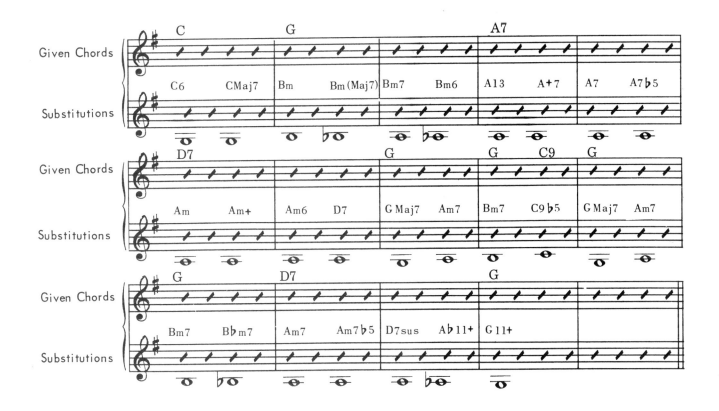

LESSON 36

The 13♭9 Chord (Fifth in Bass) and the Augmented 7♭9 Chord (Root on 5th String)
(May Be Treated as a Dominant-Type Chord in Substitutions)

Exercise on the 13♭9 and the Augmented 7♭9

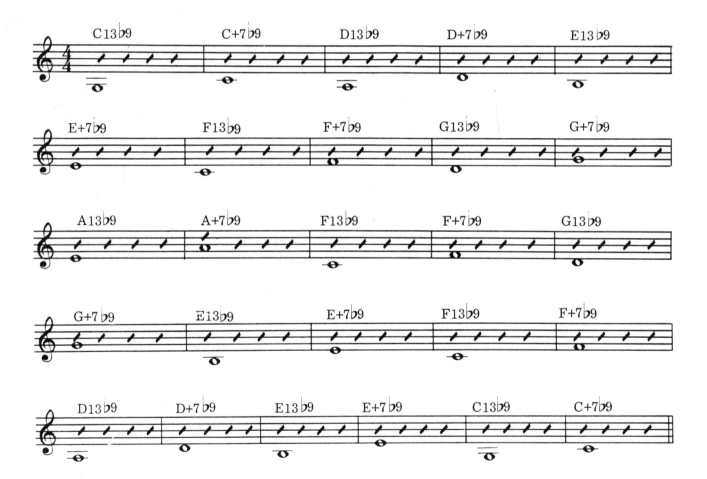

Exercise Based Upon a Well-Known Chord Progression

Understand all substitutions.

LESSON 37

SUBSTITUTIONS

The dominant 7♭9 chord fingering is exactly the same as the diminished fingering. For example, the C7♭9 with the 5th in the bass is the same as the G diminished with the G in the bass. As a result, whenever a 7♭9 chord appears, we may count up a 5th and play a diminished chord.

$$C7♭9 \quad \text{play G diminished}$$

$$A7♭9 \quad \text{play E diminished}$$

$$E7♭9 \quad \text{play B diminished}$$

By the same token, whenever a diminished chord appears, we may count down a 5th and play a dominant 7♭9 chord.

$$\text{G diminished} \quad \text{play C7♭9}$$

$$\text{E diminished} \quad \text{play A7♭9}$$

$$\text{B diminished} \quad \text{play E7♭9}$$

The 7♭9 is an alteration of the dominant 9 chord and may be used as a direct substitution for the dominant 9. In turn, the dominant 9 may at times be substituted for the 7♭9.

$$C7♭9 \quad \text{play C9}$$

$$A7♭9 \quad \text{play A9}$$

$$E7♭9 \quad \text{play E9}$$

Therefore: When a diminished chord appears it is at times acceptable to count down a 5th and play a dominant 9. When we do this we are actually substituting for a substitution. The 7♭9 is a substitution for the diminished, and the dominant 9 is a substitution for the 7♭9.

Below is a very common chord progression. The explanation above will clarify the usage of the E♭9 chord in substitution progression number 2. Bear in mind that G diminished, on the given chord line, is the same as *B♭ diminished,* D♭ diminished, and E diminished.

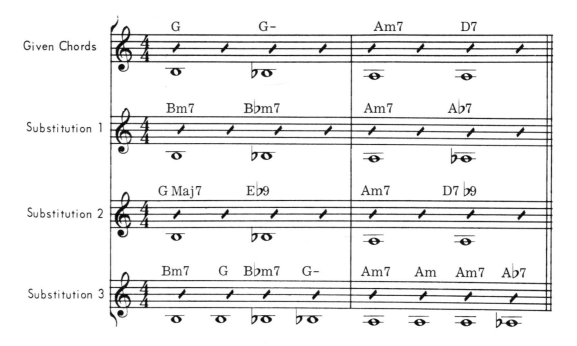

100

Below is another very common chord progression. The preceding explanation will clarify the usage of the E9 chord in the substitution progression. Bear in mind that G♯ diminished, on the given chord line, is the same as *B diminished,* D diminished, and F diminished.

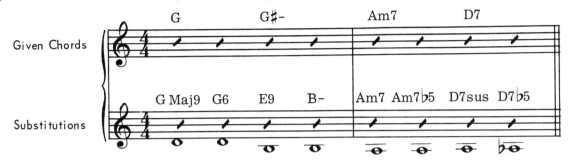

The student should analyze the substitution progressions shown in this lesson and then should attempt to apply the substitution progressions to various keys.

When passing from a major chord to a dominant 7 chord, which is a 6th higher than the major, we may use as a passing chord a minor form which is one tone lower than the dominant 7.

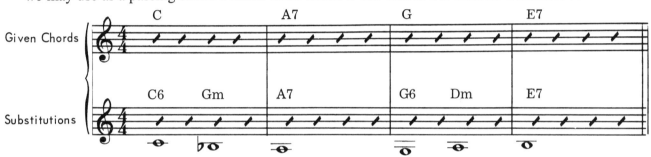

It is acceptable to play a minor 6 chord in place of a minor chord.

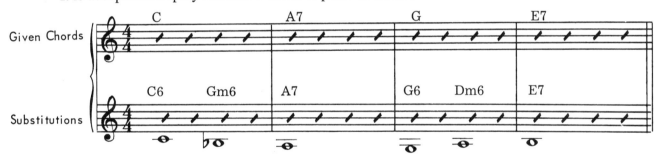

For an even prettier effect, we may use a minor 6 form, with the 6th in the bass.

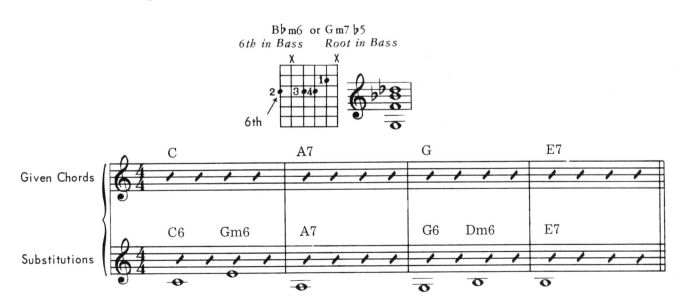

101

LESSON 38

COMMON TONES

The basis for all substitutions is common tones. In order for a chord substitution to be correct, it should contain at least one note which is also contained in the given chord. The given chord and the substitution chord should have at least one note in common.

If the given chord contains two notes which are the same as two notes in the substitution chord, then we may say that the given chord and the substitution have two common tones. The substitution chord should not be in dissonance with the melody except occasionally in brief passing.

All substitutions shown in this method stem from common tones. With time, experience, and practice, the student will be able to apply common tones with ease and will acquire even greater versatility in chord substitution.

Common Tone Examples on the Dominant 7 with the Fifth in the Bass

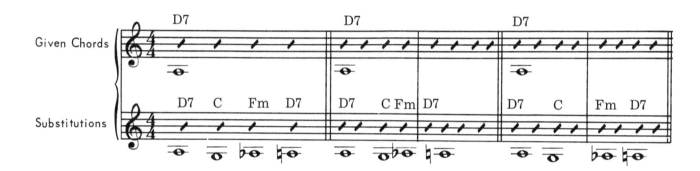

Common Tone Examples on the Dominant 7 with the Root in the Bass

(Use three-string chords on the substitution line.)

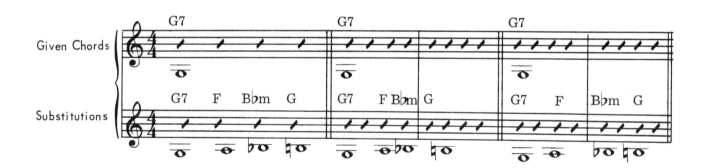

It is suggested that the student memorize the examples above and apply them to all dominant 7 chords, using both examples based on the 5th-in-the-bass dominant 7 and the root-in-the-bass dominant 7. The student should also practice applying the substitutions above to any popular music of his or her choice.

Common Tones Used for Substitutions on a Blues Progression

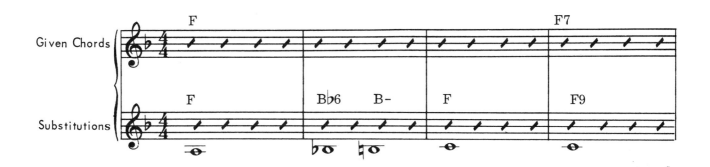

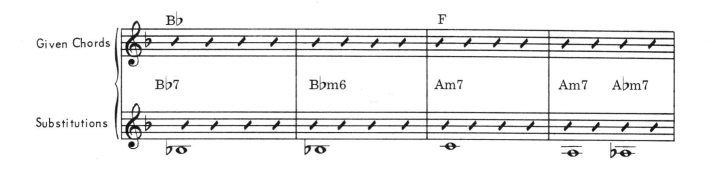

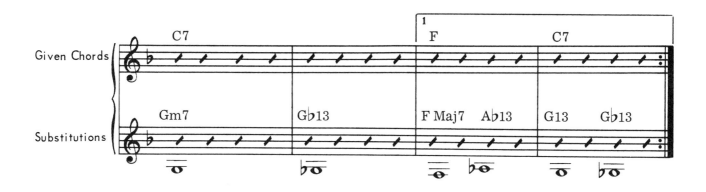

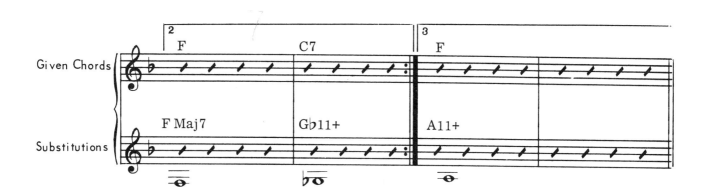

LESSON 39

APPLYING COMMON TONES TO SONG ENDINGS (ON KNOWN MELODY LINES)

Technically speaking, any substitution chord may be played for a given chord, *provided that the melody note is contained within the substitution chord(s)*. When this occurs, the melody note is the common tone which appears in both the melody and the chord(s).

Because there is generally considerable movement (from one melody note to another) in most song melodies, this means of substitution is impractical except on sustained melody notes. Another factor is that not all substitutions conceived in this manner will fit the mood of the melody or provide the desired musical effect.

However, for all of its disadvantages, the use of the melody as a common tone for the substitution chord is responsible for some of the prettiest substitutions ever conceived.

The arranger who wishes to write a modern chord accompaniment may well apply the following material. The guitarist should thoroughly understand all of the following substitutions and should apply them to various popular songs and jazz standards.

In order to better understand this manner of substitution, we will work with endings in the key of C. Since the last note of the melody line in the key of C is usually a C note, we may use as a substitution any chord(s) which contains the C note.

Chords Which Contain the Note C

Root Name	Type Name
C	Anything
D♭	Major 7, major 9, minor (maj7)
D	7, 9, 7♯9, 7♭9, aug7, 7♭5, aug7♯9, aug7♭9, aug9, 13, any dominant 7 alteration
E♭	6, min6, 6 add 9, 13, 13♭9, min6 add 9
E	Aug, aug7, aug9, aug7♭9, aug7♯9
F	Anything *except* diminished, augmented, augmented 7 or ♭5-type chords
G♭	Augmented 11, 7♭5
G	Suspended
A♭	Major anything, dominant 7 anything
A	Minor anything
B♭	9, aug9, 9 add 6
B	♭9

Below are examples showing chords containing the C note being used against a C note in the melody. For best results, the substitution chords should ultimately resolve to a C major-type chord when playing in a C major key. In a minor key, the resolution should be to a minor-type chord.

EXAMPLE 1:

EXAMPLE 2:

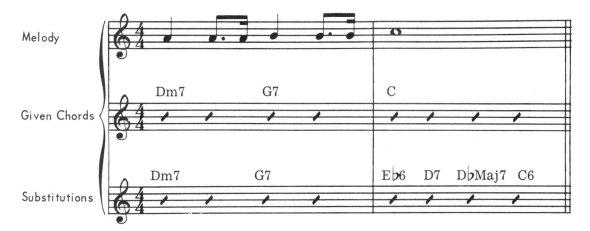

EXAMPLE 3:

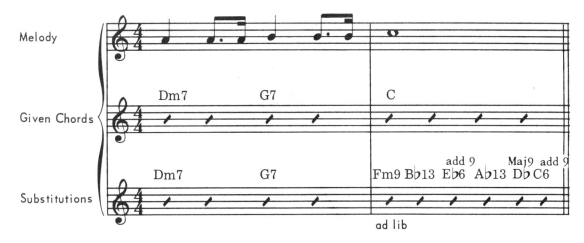

105

EXAMPLE 4:

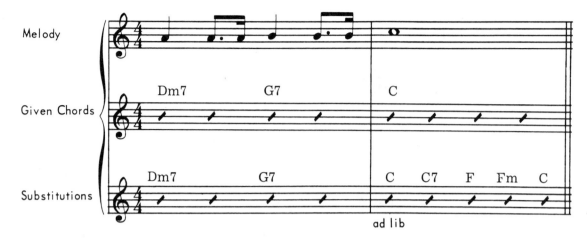

EXAMPLE 5:

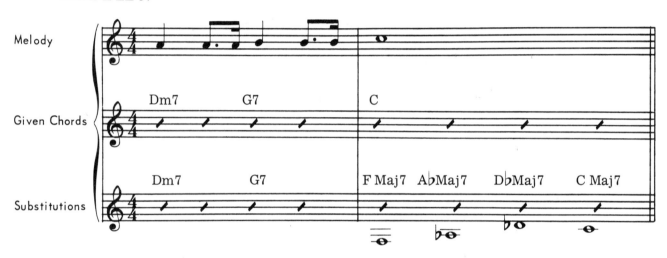

In Example 5, above, we substituted Fmaj7, A♭maj7, D♭maj7, and Cmaj7 for the given C major chord by virtue of the common tone C. The student will observe that it would have been equally acceptable to play Fmaj6, A♭maj6, D♭maj6, and Cmaj6 in place of the major 7 chords. However, the replacement of the major 7 chords by major 6 chords would add nothing to the improvement of the measure. *But if we were to use* both *the major 7* and *the major 6 chords, our substitution would be much more interesting. To attain a still more interesting effect, we may use in place of the major 6 chord the 6th* note *of the major chord. See Example 6 below.

EXAMPLE 6:

If the guitarist desires, he or she may play substitution Example 6 descending rather than ascending. See Example 7.

EXAMPLE 7:

The student should work out several endings and should then memorize them in all keys.

LESSON 40

As mentioned in an earlier lesson, any substitution chord may be used in place of a given chord provided it contains at least one of the notes in the original chord and ultimately resolves to the tonic.

EXAMPLE 1:

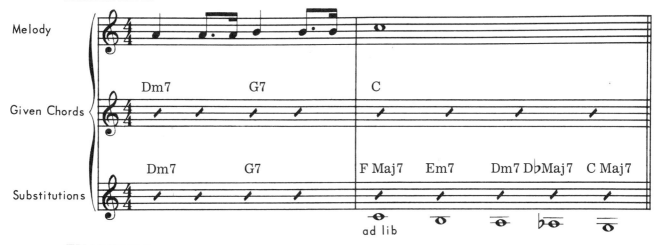

EXAMPLE 2:

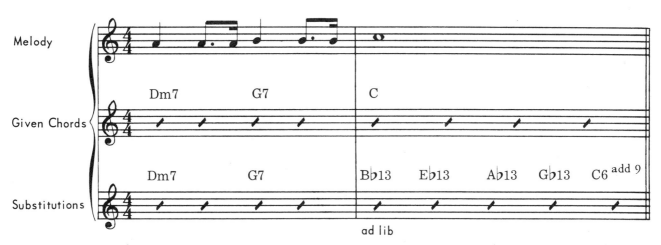

EXAMPLE 3:

Additional substitution information: It is acceptable to play a substitution chord which contains no common tones, provided that the substitution chord is one half tone above or one half tone below a chord containing a common tone(s) and also provided that the chord resolves quickly to a common tone-containing chord.

EXAMPLE:

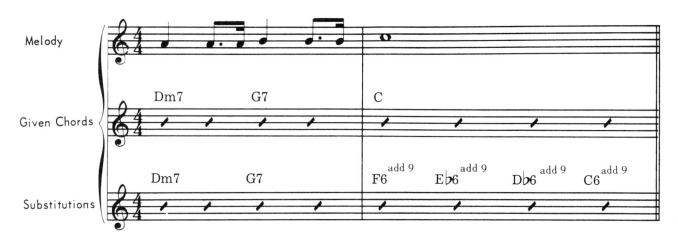

The student should apply all of his or her substitution knowledge to as many different songs as possible.

LESSON 41
PLAYING CHORD ACCOMPANIMENTS BY EAR

In musicians' slang, the playing of music by ear, whether it be melody or accompaniment, is referred to as *faking*.

Although with time and experience many musicians acquire the skill of faking, it is possible to hasten the process by becoming aware of the basic concepts of chord progression. A knowledge of "how" chords progress will prove to be of great value in learning to fake.

Broken down to its simplest form, chords progress by the cycle of 4ths. If an A-type chord should appear, then the next chord would usually be a 4th higher, or a D-type chord. If a C-type chord should appear, then the next chord would usually be a 4th higher, or an F-type chord.

For purposes of explanation, we will use the key of F major. When the student acquires sufficient ability at faking in the key of F major, he or she may transpose that knowledge to all other keys.

Our basic progression would be the tonic chord followed by a dominant 7 which is one half step below the tonic; this is followed by a series of dominant 7 chord progressing by 4ths until the tonic reappears.

1	F	E7	A7	D7	G7	C7	F

We may derive more progressions simply by omitting the 2nd chord of the progression.

2	F	A7	D7	G7	C7	F
3	F	D7	G7	C7	F	
4	F	G7	C7	F		
5	F	C7	F			

If the guitarist wishes to find the chords to a song, he or she will first try progression 1. If that doesn't work, he or she will try progression 2, and so on.

At times the progression will work well except that one chord will not seem correct. It is possible that the dissonant chord is of the proper root name but should be a minor form instead of a dominant 7.

The student should play the above progressions over and over until he or she becomes familiar with the sound of the progressions. The student should then attempt applying the progressions to songs.

In addition to the preceding progressions, there are others. If none of the five progressions fits to a song, there is a possibility that one of the progressions below will be the desired one.

6	F	B♭	F								
7	F	F7	B♭	B♭m	F	C7	F				
8	F	F7	B♭	B♭m	F	D7	G7	C7	F		
9	F	F7	B♭	B♭m	F	E7	E♭7	D7	G7	C7	F
10	F	Fdim	B♭	C7	F						
11	F	Fdim	Gm7	C7	F						
12	F	F♯dim	B♭	C7	F						
13	F	F♯dim	Gm7	C7	F						

When applying progressions to faking, a progression may not necessarily be completed. It is quite common for a progression to stop abruptly in the middle and then commence to the middle of another progression.

The student should analyze the chord progressions in many songs in order to understand how chords progress, and then attempt to play songs by ear. If the student is stymied by a chord, he or she should endeavor to find out which is the correct chord so that this knowledge may be applied to other songs. With practice, the student will become proficient at faking.

LESSON 42

COMPING

Comping, which is also referred to as chord feeding, is a manner of rhythm accompaniment playing in which the guitar player injects chords in a rhythmically ad lib style against the rhythmic beat of the music.

For example, if this should appear:

the guitarist, instead of striking the chord once for each indicated beat, may play the four bars above, something like this:

EXAMPLE 1

or like this:

EXAMPLE 2

It should be noted that it is sometimes acceptable to anticipate the chords by playing them a fraction of a second before they actually appear in the given music. In Example 1, the first measure and the third measure contain chords which are played one half beat before they appear on the "Given Chords" line. Also see Example 2, second measure.

Below is another example of comping as applied to a blues progression.

The guitarist should play the blues progression over and over. Each time the progression is played, it should be comped differently. Compings should never be memorized but should be applied in a completely extemporaneous manner.

By listening to others comp and by practicing comping with chord substitution, the guitarist will experience no great difficulty in mastering the technique of comping in a relatively short period of time.

LESSON 43

The following are additional chords which the guitarist should memorize and use. It may be argued that the following chords and, for that matter, many of the chords which were covered in the preceding pages, will rarely be seen in a guitar part. This is all very true. However, the altered chords are ideal when used as substitutions. When using altered chords, the harmonic substitution possibilities are virtually limitless.

All of the chords which are used in this method are chosen because they contain the best and most practical voicings possible. It should be noted that the best voicing does not necessarily require that the chord fingering contain every note of the chord. What is of importance, however, is that the chord "sound" be established. Those who have completed this book will agree that a properly voiced three-note chord can produce more drive and interest than a poorly voiced six-string chord.

The guitarist who correctly employs chords and substitutions will find that each chord smoothly leads into the next chord. Smooth voice leading will automatically occur as a result of using correctly voiced chords and substitutions. If all of the substitution rules are carried out to the letter but chord voicings are used which are other than those presented, it is likely that good voice leading may be lacking.

The dominant eleventh chord is absent in this book because this writer believes that a dominant seventh suspended will serve equally as well. This book does not contain every possible chord. This is because of the almost infinite amount of chord alterations. However, the guitarist at this point should be capable of deriving every possible chord, and voicing it to produce the very best chordal effect. By categorizing each chord as either a major-type, minor-type, or a dominant-type chord, there should be no difficulty applying chord substitutions.

The guitarist will find that there is much work ahead in perfecting and expanding upon all of the principles set forth in this course.

In closing, I hope that you have found this jazz method interesting, enlightening, and a means to moving forward in the fascinating field of chord accompaniment.

Ronny Lee

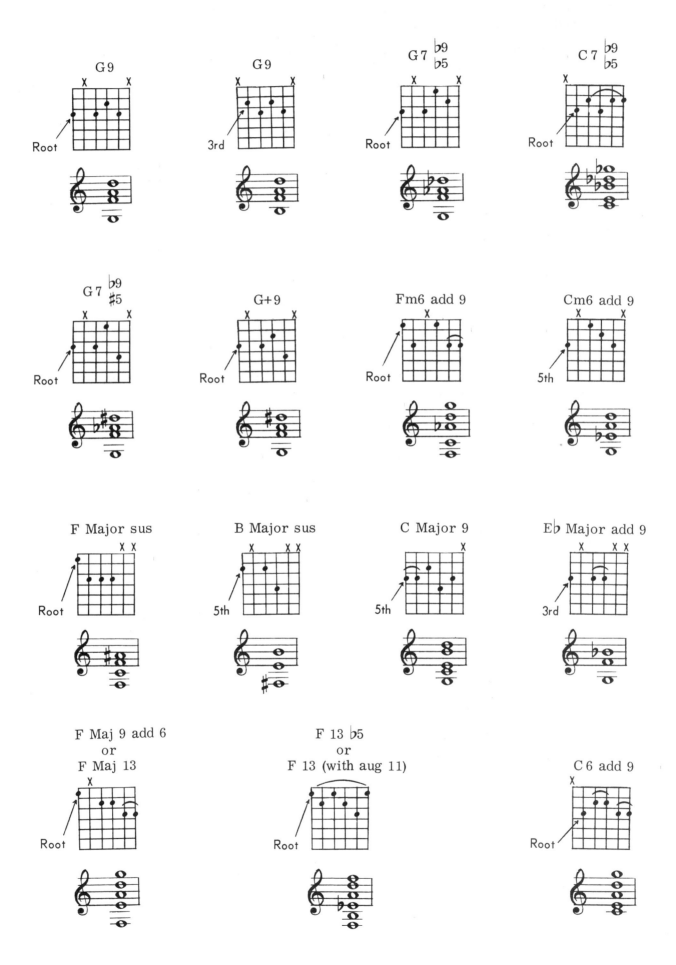